SECRETS OF SPACE

by

Ian Ridpath

Edited by Bill Bruce

Illustrated by Ron Jobson

Ray Rourke Publishing Company, Inc.
Windermere, Florida 32786

Published by Ray Rourke Publishing Company, Inc.,
Windermere, Florida 32786.
Copyright © 1980 Piper Books Ltd.
Copyright © 1981 Ray Rourke Publishing Company, Inc.
All rights reserved. No part of this book may
be reprinted or utilized in any form or by any
means, electronic or mechanical including
photocopying, recording or by any information
storage and retrieval system, without permission
in writing from the publisher.

Library of Congress Cataloging in Publication Data

Ridpath, Ian.
  Secrets of space.

  Includes index.
  SUMMARY: Discusses the planets of our solar
system, the behavior of stars, and milestones in
space exploration.
  1. Astronomy—Juvenile literature.
2. Astronautics—Juvenile literature.   [1. Astronomy.   2. Astronautics]   I. Bruce, Bill.   II. Jobson, Ron.   III. Title.
QB46.R53   1981   500.5   81-113
ISBN 0-444-86163-7   AACR1

Contents

	page		page
The Earth in Space	4	Stardeath	24
The Moon	6	Special Stars	26
Mercury	8	The Milky Way	28
Venus	9	Origin of the Universe	30
Mars	10	How we Know	32
Jupiter	12	Rockets	34
Saturn	14	Satellites	36
Uranus	16	Space Probes	38
Neptune	16	Man in Space	40
Pluto	17	Space Stations	42
Debris in Space	18	New Era in Space	44
The Sun	20	The Future	46
Life of a Star	22	Index	48

The Earth in Space

We live on a small planet called the Earth, one of nine planets which orbit the Sun. The Earth is the third planet in line from the Sun, lying at a distance of approximately 93 million miles. The Sun and its family of planets, along with various smaller pieces of orbiting debris, make up the solar system.

The four planets closest to the Sun—Mercury, Venus, Earth and Mars—are all small, rocky bodies. Farther from the Sun lie four planets made mostly of gas—Jupiter, Saturn, Uranus and Neptune. At the edge of the solar system is Pluto, a small, frozen world with an erratic orbit that weaves in and out across the path of Neptune. Orbiting between the planets are chunks of rock and metal called asteroids, and loose collections of rock and frozen gas called comets.

What is the difference between a planet and a star? A planet is a body that does not give out light of its own, whereas stars glow of their own accord. The planets of our solar system shine by reflecting light from the Sun. All the planets out as far as Saturn are visible to the unaided eye, but the planets beyond Saturn, seem fainter because they are farther away, and need a telescope to be seen.

By contrast, stars can be seen over vast distances because they are self-luminous balls of gas, generating heat and light by nuclear reactions at their centers. The Sun is a typical star. It appears much bigger and brighter than the stars we see at night simply because it is much closer than they are.

The nearest star to the Sun, Alpha Centauri, is over 25 million million miles away. Other stars are farther away still. Distances between stars are so great that they are measured not in miles but in light-years, the distance that a beam of light (which moves at 186,000 miles per second) travels in a year. A light-year is equivalent to nearly 6 million million miles, and thus Alpha Centauri is said to be 4.3 light years away.

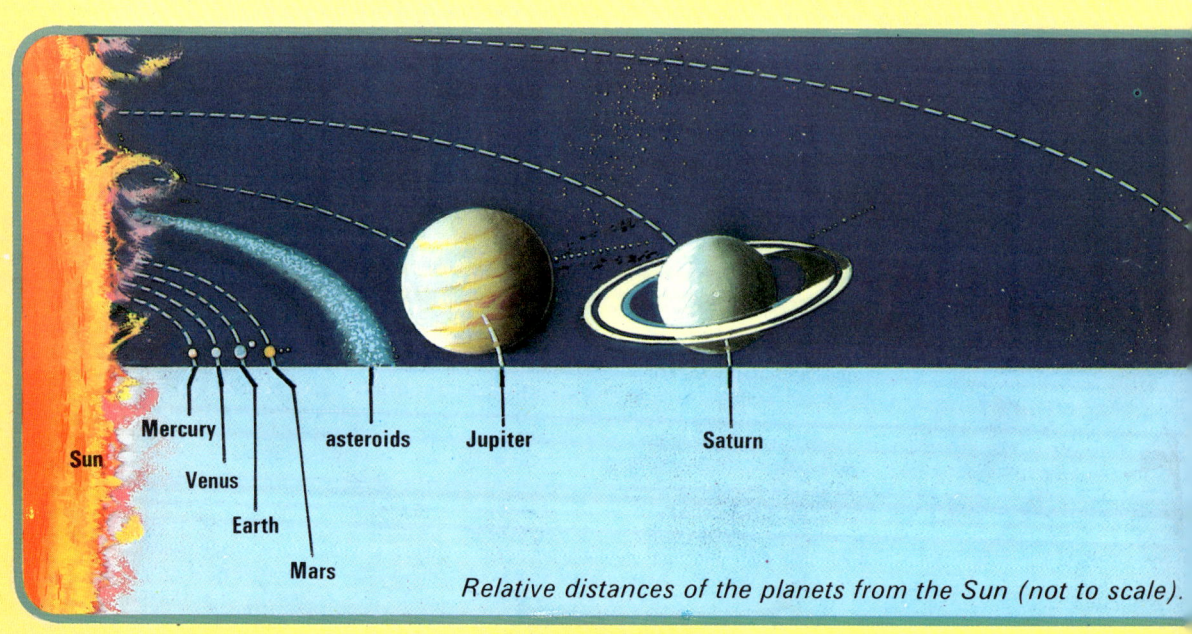

Relative distances of the planets from the Sun (not to scale).

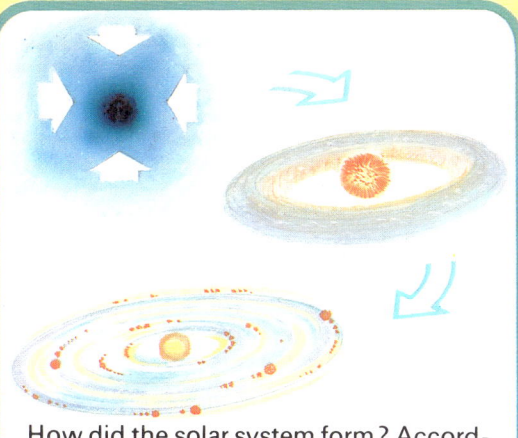

How did the solar system form? According to current ideas, the planets were born about 4,700 million years ago from a cloud of gas and dust orbiting the Sun. Slowly, over millions of years, the specks of dust in the cloud collided and stuck together, building up into large lumps of material, while most of the gas was lost into space. Gravity pulled these larger lumps of rock and metal together, forming planets. Most of the remaining debris was swept up in collisions although some still orbits the Sun today in the form of comets, asteroids and meteorites.

There may be planets around other stars in space, but they would be too faint for us to see with our present equipment. Astronomers hope that one day they may be able to detect planets of other stars, perhaps with the help of big telescopes in space.

The Earth is a rocky ball 7,900 miles in diameter. Three-quarters of its surface is covered with water, and it is surrounded by an atmosphere of gas. As seen from space, the Earth appears blue and white—the blue being water and the white being clouds. Life on Earth needs air and water to survive.

The Earth is never still in space. It spins on its axis in 24 hours, a period we call one day. At the same time it is orbiting the Sun. One orbit around the Sun takes about $365\frac{1}{4}$ days to complete, and is called a year.

The Earth is not alone in space. It has a natural satellite, called the Moon. All other planets, except Mercury and Venus, have moons, too.

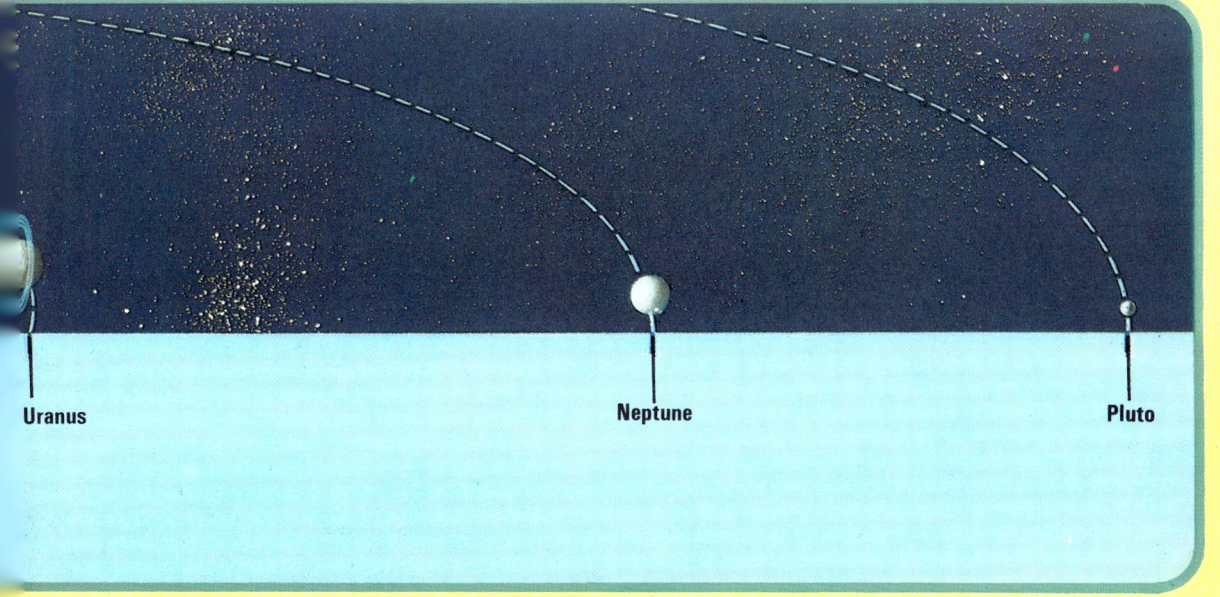

Uranus   Neptune   Pluto

The Moon

The Moon is the Earth's companion and nearest neighbor in space. It is a rocky body without air or water, 2,160 miles in diameter, about one quarter the size of the Earth. The Moon lies 239,000 miles from us, which is very close on the scale of the solar system.

The Moon orbits the Earth about once a month—in fact, the word "month" comes from "moon". Early calendars were based on the motion of the Moon around the Earth, but in our modern calendar the lengths of the months have been altered somewhat and no longer correspond exactly with the Moon's orbital motion.

As the Moon orbits the Earth it keeps one face permanently turned towards us. Until the advent of the space age, no one had seen the Moon's far side. Now, space probes have shown that it is covered with craters and rugged mountains, and is even rougher than the near side.

Because the Moon is close to us it was a natural target for astronauts. In the American Apollo programme, six teams of astronauts landed on the Moon to collect rocks and explore its surface. The first landing, by Neil Armstrong and Edwin Aldrin, was made in July 1969, and the last in December 1972.

From the rock samples the astronauts brought back, geologists have found that the dark lowland plains of the Moon are at least 3,000 million years old, and the brightest highlands are older still. Evidently, the Moon was heavily bombarded from space early in its history, when most of the craters were formed, but for the past 3,000 million years it has remained relatively unchanged.

One question that the Apollo landings did not solve was the origin of the Moon. There are three theories. One is that the Moon is a part of the Earth that broke off. Another theory is that the Moon was a passing body that was captured by the Earth's gravitational pull, while a third theory is that the Earth and Moon formed side by side and have therefore always been together. Most astronomers favor the third theory, but ideas could change when more information becomes available. One day, men will return to the Moon to continue their exploration of our neighbor in space.

Even a small pair of binoculars shows that the surface of the Moon is pockmarked with craters of all sizes, up to 140 miles or more in diameter. There are also dark lowland plains, which make up the familiar Man-in-the-Moon figure seen by the naked eye.

Astronomers argued for centuries over the origin of these craters on the Moon. Some said they were giant volcanoes while others maintained that they were formed by meteorites smashing into the Moon. Today, most astronomers agree that the largest craters were caused by impacts from meteorites but there may also be some small volcanoes on the Moon.

Volcanic lava apparently once flooded into the low lying regions of the Moon, forming the dark lunar plains.

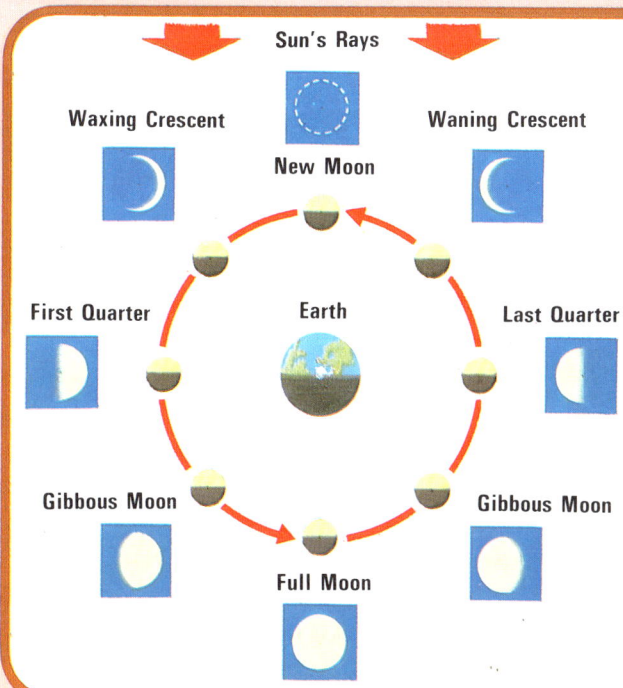

As the Moon orbits the Earth it goes through its familiar cycle of phases, from new Moon (completely invisible) to full Moon and back to new again. Half the Moon is always illuminated by the Sun but the Moon's phase depends on how much of that illuminated half is visible to us.

When the Moon is close to the Sun in the sky, all the illuminated portion is turned away from us and the Moon is invisible (new Moon). As the Moon moves around the Earth we at first see a thin crescent, and then a half-illuminated Moon. When the Moon is opposite the Sun in the sky we see it fully illuminated (full Moon).

As the Moon moves from new to full it is said to be waxing. As it moves back to new Moon again it is said to be waning.

Mercury

Mercury, the closest known planet to the Sun, is a small, rocky body 3,100 miles in diameter, only 50 per cent larger than our own Moon. It is difficult to see properly from Earth because it keeps so close to the Sun. Astronomers had to wait until the Mariner 10 space probe flew past Mercury in 1974 to get a good look at its surface.

Mercury looks like the Moon. It is scarred by numerous craters caused by bombardment from meteorites, plus lowland plains that appear to have been flooded by volcanic lava.

Conditions on Mercury are extreme. It has no air or water. On the side facing the Sun, the surface temperature rises to 415°C, hot enough to melt tin and lead. On the side turned away from the Sun, the temperature falls to a chilling 175°C below zero. Bathed in dangerous radiation from the Sun, the planet must be far too hostile for any form of life and would be very unhealthy for astronauts to visit.

Mercury orbits the Sun every 88 days at an average distance of 36 million miles. It rotates on its axis very slowly, every 59 days. The gravitational pull of the Sun acts as a brake on Mercury's rate of spin.

Occasionally, Mercury is seen passing across the face of the Sun, an event known as a transit. In transit, Mercury appears as a small black spot against the glaring Sun. The next transit will occur in 1986.

Venus

Venus, the second planet in line from the Sun (67.2 million miles) was until recently a mystery planet, shrouded in unbroken cloud which prevented astronomers from seeing its surface. These clouds reflect the Sun's light strongly, making Venus the most brilliant planet visible from Earth. It is often seen as the so-called morning or evening "star".

Theories suggested that under its clouds Venus might be covered in water, that it might be a dust bowl, or that it might have lush vegetation and creatures like prehistoric monsters.

With a diameter of 7,700 miles, Venus is similar in size to the Earth, but there the similarity ends. Probes have found that it is unbearably hostile.

Its atmosphere is made almost entirely of unbreathable carbon dioxide gas. This traps heat from the Sun like a blanket, forcing temperatures to a furnace-like 475°C both day and night. The atmosphere bears down with a crushing pressure 90 times that of the Earth's atmosphere. The famous clouds are not made of water vapor, like the clouds of Earth, but consist of concentrated sulphuric acid. Anyone who went there would be crushed, roasted, suffocated and corroded.

There is one remaining puzzle about Venus. It rotates on its axis back to front—that is, from east to west, the opposite direction from the Earth and other planets. It does so every 243 days, which is longer than the 225 days it takes to orbit the Sun. No one knows why it is so out of step.

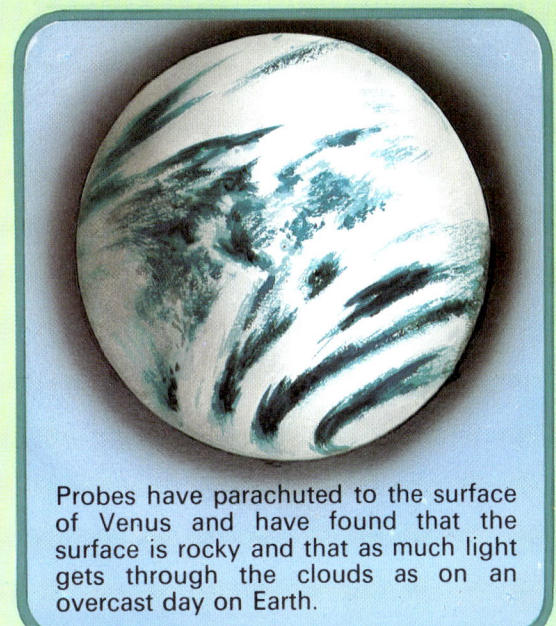

Probes have parachuted to the surface of Venus and have found that the surface is rocky and that as much light gets through the clouds as on an overcast day on Earth.

Mars

Mars, the planet next in line from the Sun, has intrigued people for generations because of the possibility that it might support life.

Mars is about half the size of the Earth, with a diameter of 4,200 miles. It orbits the Sun every 687 days at an average distance of 141.5 million miles. Astronomers saw that the day on Mars lasted only slightly longer than our own, and that the planet had an atmosphere in which clouds formed, plus white polar caps. Could it therefore be similar to the Earth, even harboring life?

The astronomer, Percival Lowell thought that he saw canals on Mars, perhaps used by Martians to bring water from the polar caps to their crops at the equator. Other astronomers could not see them and probes have shown that they do not exist.

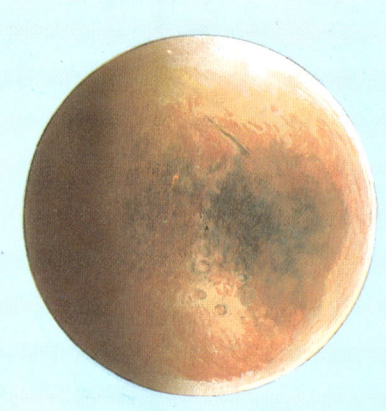

Mars is often known as the red planet, because of its distinctive color, caused by extensive desert areas and dust in the atmosphere.

Mars has two small moons, Phobos and Deimos. They are irregular-shaped lumps of rock, approximately 14 miles and 7 miles across respectively, looking rather like battered potatoes.

Phobos and Deimos are probably former asteroids that were captured by the gravitational pull of Mars.

Viking landers photographed the red, desert-like surface of Mars while a miniature on-board laboratory tested the soil for signs of life.

Space probes have found that Mars has craters on its surface. Some of the craters were apparently formed by the impact of meteorites, but others are undoubtedly volcanoes. The largest of these, called Olympus Mons (Mount Olympus) is 310 miles wide and 12 miles high, making it the largest known volcano in the solar system. There is also a gigantic rift valley on Mars, 2,500 miles long and up to 75 miles wide. Evidently this was caused by a fault in the planet's crust and has subsequently been eroded by wind-blown dust.

Mars has turned out to be less welcoming than previously thought. Its atmosphere, made of carbon dioxide, is as thin as the air 20 miles above the Earth. Even on a summer afternoon, temperatures at the surface of Mars do not rise above freezing point.

Photographs taken by probes orbiting Mars showed no sign of life on the planet, not even patches of vegetation. But that did not rule out the possibility of small plants such as cacti on the surface, or creatures living in the soil. The only way to find out was to land and look...

Olympus Mons

Martian Rift Valley

In 1976, two Viking space probes landed on Mars to look for life. Their cameras showed the surface to be a red-colored stony desert. The sky is pink, caused by dust in the atmosphere.

Viking carried on board an automatic biology laboratory, which tested samples of Martian soil to see if any tiny bugs or bacteria were living in it. No definite signs of anything living or growing were found. It is possible that some form of life exists on parts of Mars not visited by the Viking lander, but it does not seem very likely. Most astronomers now believe that there is no life on Mars. One day, astronauts will visit Mars and perhaps set up permanent bases there.

Jupiter

Jupiter is the giant planet of the solar system. It is a storm-tossed ball of gas enclosed by lethal zones of radiation. It weighs $2\frac{1}{2}$ times as much as all the other planets put together, with a diameter of 80,700 miles, 11 times that of the Earth. Yet it is made mostly of the lightest materials in the Universe, the gases hydrogen and helium. Its composition is very similar to that of the Sun and if Jupiter had been at least 10 times bigger and heavier, it would have begun to glow like a small star. As it is, Jupiter gives off twice as much heat as it receives from the Sun. Jupiter has been called "the star that failed".

When you look at Jupiter through a telescope you see a swirling mass of multicolored clouds around the planet, drawn out into bands by the rapid rotation of just under 10 hours, the fastest of any planet in the solar system. The colors in the clouds, mostly red, brown and yellow, are caused by traces of various chemicals in the atmosphere.

There is no solid surface under the clouds, instead, the gases of which Jupiter is made get denser and denser until they are compressed into liquid. Jupiter is mostly a ball of liquid hydrogen and helium, although there may be a small core of rocky material at the very center. Probes entering the clouds of Jupiter would eventually be crushed by the immense pressures. Jupiter orbits the Sun every 11.9 years at a distance of 483.4 million miles.

There is only one permanent feature in the ever-changing clouds of Jupiter. It is aptly named the great red spot and is oval in shape and big enough to swallow three Earths laid side by side. It is usually red in color but can also appear pink or brown.

The red spot was first seen through telescopes in 1666. At first, some astronomers thought it might be the gaping vent of a fiery volcano, but that theory was soon dismissed. More recent theories suggested it could be an object floating in the clouds.

Pictures from the two Voyager space probes in 1979 cleared up the mystery by showing the red spot to be nothing more than a spinning whirlpool of cloud. Other whirling spots of various colors appear in the clouds of Jupiter from time to time, but none is as big as the great red spot and none lasts so long.

Jupiter has a family of at least 13 moons. The four largest moons, first seen by the Italian scientist Galileo Galilei in 1610, can be seen in even a simple pair of binoculars. Two of these moons, Ganymede and Callisto, are larger than the planet Mercury. The Voyager space probes in 1979 discovered impact craters and ice patches on Ganymede and Callisto. Most startlingly, volcanoes were spotted erupting on another moon, Io, whose surface is covered with orange and yellow deposits of salt and sulfur. The Voyager probes also found that Jupiter is encircled by a thin ring of rocky debris, too faint to be seen from Earth.

Saturn

Saturn is widely regarded as the most beautiful planet in the solar system, because of the system of bright rings that surrounds it. These rings are not solid, as they may at first appear, but consist of tiny moonlets orbiting the planet.

Apart from its rings, Saturn is a scaled-down version of Jupiter. The two planets are made of much the same materials – mostly hydrogen and helium gas. But the clouds surrounding Saturn are not as turbulent or colorful as those of stormy Jupiter.

Saturn is second in size to Jupiter, being 75,000 miles in diameter and is also second to Jupiter in speed of rotation, spinning every $10\frac{1}{4}$ hours. Saturn takes $29\frac{1}{2}$ years to orbit the Sun at a distance of 886 million miles. It is the most distant planet visible with the naked eye.

Saturn is unique in one respect. The gases of which it is made are not as densely compressed as the gases of Jupiter and, in fact, Saturn has an overall density less than that of water. Therefore, given a big enough ocean, the giant planet would float!

Saturn's rings were first seen by the Italian scientist Galileo Galilei with his small telescope in 1610. Astronomers took some time to work out the exact nature of the rings. We now know that they consist of chunks of rock about the size of bricks, orbiting the planet and probably representing the building blocks of a moon that never formed. These particles of rock are coated with ice, which makes them appear very bright. Saturn's rings were once thought to be unique but rings have now been discovered around Jupiter and Uranus.

Saturn's rings extend for 170,000 miles from rim to rim, yet their thickness from top to bottom is only about 6 miles. Seen edge on, therefore, they are almost invisible. In relation to their diameter, the rings of Saturn are thinner than a sheet of paper.

The outermost part of the rings is called Ring A. It is separated from the brightest and widest part of the rings, Ring B, by a 1,700-mile gap called Cassini's division, named after the French astronomer who detected it in 1675. The thin Ring C, also known as the crepe ring, lies inside Ring B. Closer still to the planet lies a faint fourth ring.

Saturn has at least 10 moons, the largest of which is Titan. Titan is particularly interesting as it is 3,600 miles in diameter and is the only satellite known to have a substantial atmosphere. Titan appears to be shrouded by dense clouds, possibly similar to the clouds around Saturn and Jupiter.

Uranus

Until 1781, the solar system was believed to stop at Saturn. That year, the English astronomer William Herschel discovered a new planet. It was named Uranus.

Uranus is a ball of gas 29,200 miles in diameter. It appears greenish because its atmosphere contains large amounts of methane.

Uranus orbits the Sun every 84 years at a distance of 1,782 million miles. The planet's axis is tilted on its side, as though it has been knocked over in a massive collision and, as a result, seasons on Uranus are extreme. Each pole experiences a 42-year summer and a 42-year winter. Uranus is so difficult to observe that we do not know exactly how fast it spins.

In 1977, astronomers discovered that Uranus is encircled by faint rings of rocky debris. Nine rings are now known to exist and are believed to be the remains of a moon that broke up. Five moons of Uranus have been discovered.

Neptune

Once Uranus had been discovered, astronomers started to search for other planets deep in the solar system. In 1845, they were rewarded with the discovery of another giant planet, Neptune. This turned out to be a near twin of Uranus. Like Uranus, Neptune appears greenish in color because of methane gas in its cloudy atmosphere. Under their atmospheres both planets are believed to have large, rocky cores coated with thick ice.

Neither Uranus nor Neptune show any bands or other markings in their clouds, so it has not been possible to measure their speeds of rotation with any accuracy. Both planets, however, are believed to spin more slowly than Jupiter or Saturn. Neptune has two known moons.

Neptune is 2,792 million miles away from the Sun and takes 165 years to complete one orbit.

Pluto

At the outer edge of the solar system is the most baffling planet of all, Pluto. So small and faint is Pluto that it was not discovered until 1930, as the result of a photographic search for new planets.

Pluto is now believed to be the smallest planet in the solar system, with an estimated diameter of 1,900 miles, it is smaller than our own Moon. It is probably nothing more than a ball of frozen gas. Some astronomers think Pluto is too small to be classified as a proper planet at all. One theory says it is an escaped satellite of Neptune, or it could be the largest of a distant belt of asteroids. In 1978 a moon of Pluto was discovered.

Although Pluto is on average the most distant planet from the Sun, its orbit actually crosses the path of Neptune. Therefore, for part of its 248-year orbit Pluto is closer to the Sun than Neptune. This is the case at present. From 1979 to 1999, Neptune, not Pluto, is temporarily the outermost planet of the solar system.

Pluto will be closest to the Sun, at a distance of 2,744 million miles, in 1989. At its farthest, it lies 4,573 million miles from the Sun. From this distance, the Sun appears as a small but intense point of light. Pluto's average distance from the Sun is 3,658 million miles.

Debris in Space

In addition to the major planets, the solar system contains thousands of minor planets, known as asteroids. Most asteroids orbit the Sun in a belt between Mars and Jupiter but there are some which stray across the paths of planets. If one of these wandering asteroids hit the Earth, as could happen at any time, it would cause massive devastation.

Asteroids are rubble left over from the formation of the solar system. They are made of rock and metal, like the Earth and other inner planets. The largest asteroid, Ceres, is 620 miles in diameter and orbits the Sun every 4.6 years at an average distance of 257 million miles. Ceres was the first asteroid to be discovered, in 1801.

About 2,000 asteroids have been cataloged by astronomers, ranging from the size of Ceres down to only a mile or so in diameter. There are estimated to be many thousands more small asteroids so far undiscovered.

Occasionally, lumps of rock or metal known as meteorites crash to Earth from space. Meteorites are probably fragments broken off asteroids by collisions.

If a meteorite is traveling fast enough when it strikes the ground, it can dig out an enormous crater. One such meteorite crater lies in the Arizona desert near Flagstaff. This crater, 4,150 feet in diameter, is believed to have been formed about 20,000 years ago by the impact of an iron meteorite that may have weighed as much as a quarter of a million tons. Most of the meteorite was destroyed in the blast but several tons of iron fragments scattered over the surrounding countryside. Fortunately, such major impacts are rare. Most meteorites are traveling too slowly when they hit the ground to cause much damage, although some have smashed roofs and windows.

The world's largest known meteorite lies where it fell in prehistoric times, near Grootfontein in Namibia. It is estimated to weigh over 60 tons.

The Arizona Meteorite Crater

On any clear night, you can see several so-called shooting stars flash across the heavens each hour. These are not stars at all but particles of dust burning up in the Earth's upper atmosphere. Their proper name is meteors.

A typical meteor is about the size of a grain of sand. Its dying blaze of glory lasts for less than a second. Meteors are believed to be dust from comets. Occasionally, the Earth encounters whole swarms and a so-called meteor shower takes place. Several meteor showers occur regularly each year. The most spectacular are the Perseid meteors in August, when as many as one shooting star per minute may be seen.

The Earth is sweeping up dust from space all the time. Over 10,000 tons of cosmic dust is estimated to arrive on Earth each year.

Comets are ghostly wanderers in the solar system. They consist of loose rock and dust welded together by frozen gas. Comets travel on long, looping orbits between the planets, spending much of their time in the dark and cold outer reaches of the solar system where they are invisible. When a comet approaches the Sun it begins to warm up and glow. Gas and dust stream away from its head to form a flowing tail which can be millions of miles long.

About 1,000 comets are known, the most famous of which is Halley's comet which returns to the vicinity of the Sun every 76 years. It last appeared in 1910 and is expected to return in 1986.

The Sun

The Sun is our parent star. Without its heat and light there would be no life on Earth. It is an incandescent ball of gas 864,000 miles in diameter. A line of 109 Earths would be needed to equal the diameter of the Sun and a third of a million Earths would be required to outweigh it.

The Sun is made almost entirely of hydrogen and helium gas.

The Sun's surface has a temperature of 6,000°C, but at its center temperatures rise to an unimaginable 15 million degrees.

The Sun's visible surface is called the photosphere, meaning sphere of light. Surrounding the Sun is a faint halo of thin gas called the corona, which is normally invisible. The corona can be seen with special instruments, or when the Moon blocks off light from the Sun's disk at a total eclipse.

The Sun's face is frequently blemished by spots and storms. Storms on the Sun, known as flares, throw off atomic particles which travel through space and can cause radio interference on Earth. From time to time, giant looping arches of gas, known as prominences are seen extending from the Sun's surface.

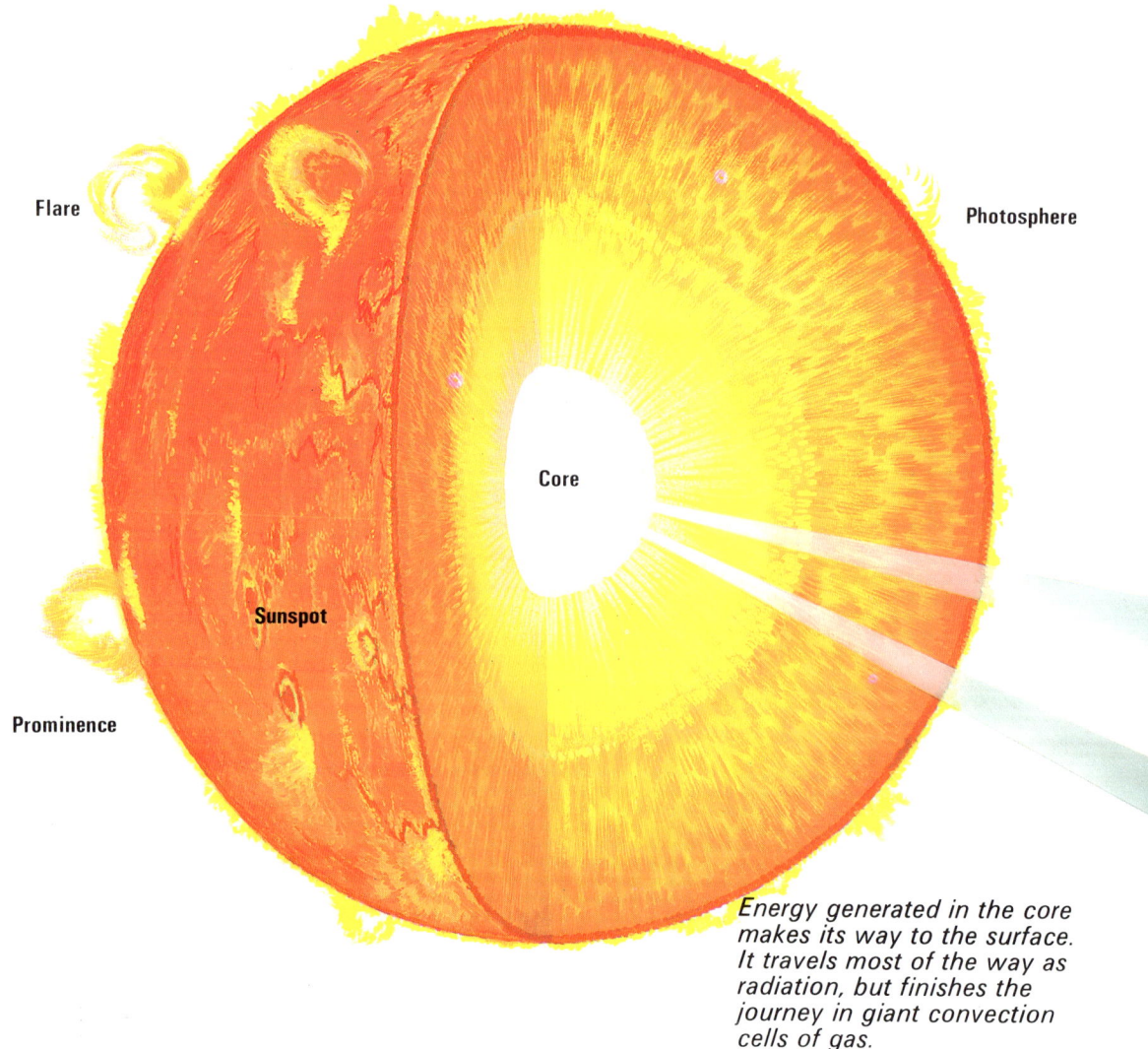

Energy generated in the core makes its way to the surface. It travels most of the way as radiation, but finishes the journey in giant convection cells of gas.

When the Moon passes in front of the Sun, it blots out the Sun's light to produce an eclipse.

If only part of the Sun is covered by the Moon, this is known as a partial eclipse. When all of the Sun's brilliant disk is blocked out, this is a total eclipse. During total eclipses, which can last five minutes or more, the sky becomes dark and the faint outer halo of the Sun, called the corona, becomes visible. About two eclipses of the Sun occur each year, but each one is visible from only a limited part of the Earth. You must be very lucky to be directly in the path of a total eclipse of the Sun and scientists will travel half way across the world to witness one.

The Moon can also be eclipsed. An eclipse of the Moon occurs when it passes into the shadow of the Earth. This usually happens about twice a year.

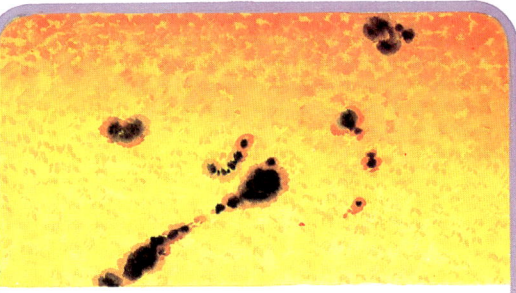

Dark patches known as sunspots are frequently seen on the face of the Sun. These are areas of cooler gas which do not glow as brightly as the surrounding photosphere. Sunspots can be enormous. Most of them are larger than the Earth and some form groups that stretch for 90,000 miles or more—half the distance from the Earth to the Moon. By watching sunspots cross the face of the Sun, astronomers have found that the Sun rotates once every 25 days at the equator but more slowly towards the poles.

The number of sunspots visible at any one time varies in a cycle that lasts about 11 years. At sunspot minimum, no spots may be seen on the Sun for days on end. But when the sun is at maximum activity, hundreds of spots may be visible at a time. Some scientists believe that sunspot activity affects weather on Earth.

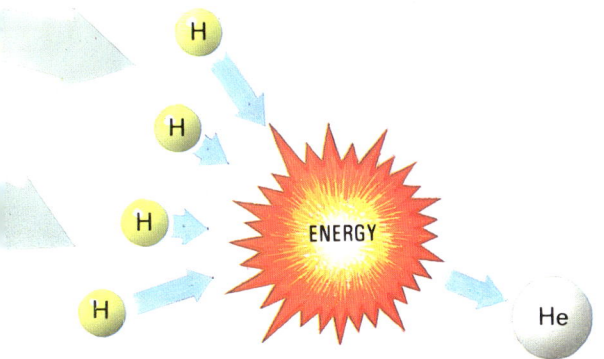

What makes the Sun glow? It does not burn like an ordinary fire. Instead, its center is like a gigantic nuclear reactor. There, in conditions of extreme pressure and temperature, reactions which release energy take place between atoms. In the reactions, four atoms of hydrogen are squeezed together to make one atom of helium. This process is known as fusion, as occurs in a hydrogen bomb. But the Sun does not blow itself to pieces because it is so big that its own gravity holds it together. These energy-giving reactions mean that the Sun is slowly turning itself from hydrogen into helium. Each second, 600 million tons of hydrogen in the Sun are fused together to become helium, with 4 million tons of hydrogen being converted into energy in the process. There is so much hydrogen in the Sun that even at this rate of energy generation it can live for 10,000 million years. It is currently about halfway through that life span.

21

Life of a Star

Stars are born from Giant clouds of gas and dust in the Galaxy. Such clouds are termed nebulas. One famous example is the Orion nebula (opposite), visible to the naked eye as a fuzzy, glowing patch in the constellation of Orion. The Orion nebula is lit by stars which have recently formed within it. Our own Sun is believed to have been born from such a cloud of matter.

A nebula like that in Orion can give rise to a whole cluster of stars. Star formation begins when parts of the cloud start to contract under the inward pull of their own gravity, forming blobs of gas. Each blob continues to contract until the temperature and pressure at its center become so extreme that nuclear reactions begin. The blob then begins to glow, giving out its own light and heat. A new star has been born. This process of star formation is believed to be going on today inside the Orion nebula and other nebulas like it.

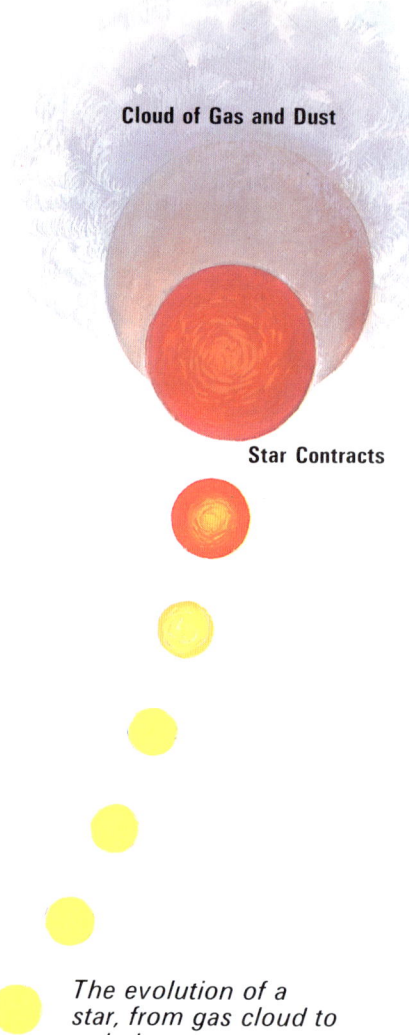

The evolution of a star, from gas cloud to red giant.

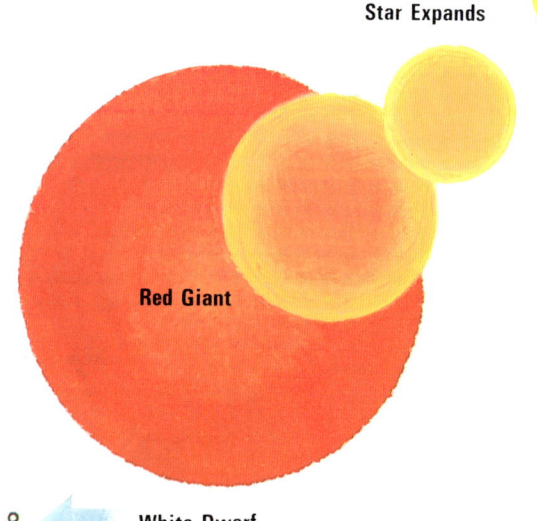

Stars spend most of their lives glowing in a steady fashion. They create energy at their centers by the fusion of hydrogen into helium in nuclear reactions.

Towards the end of its life, a star starts to use up its hydrogen fuel more quickly. When this happens, it becomes bigger and brighter, swelling into what is known as a red giant. Red giant stars, noticeable by their color, are very big and bright. An example is the star Arcturus, in the constellation

An example of a young cluster of stars in the group known as Pleiades (below), in the constellation of Taurus. About half a dozen members of the Pleiades are visible to the naked eye, but telescopes reveal that the cluster contains a total of about 200 stars. The stars of the Pleiades are still surrounded by traces of the cloud from which they were formed. The youngest stars of the Pleiades are estimated to have come into being during the past 2 million years. Our Sun was probably a member of such a cluster when it was born, 4,700 million years ago.

Boötes, the herdsman. Arcturus is one of the brightest stars in our sky. It is about 25 times the diameter of the Sun, and gives out 100 times as much light.

Arcturus is a picture of our own Sun in old age, for the Sun will one day swell into a red giant. When it does so, it will become so large that it will swallow Mercury, Venus, and possibly even the Earth.

As the Sun swells into a red giant, the Earth's climate will change dramatically. The polar ice caps will melt, flooding low lying areas, then, as temperatures continue to rise, the seas will evaporate, leaving the Earth a parched cinder.

Fortunately, the Sun is in stable middle age. It is not expected to turn into a red giant for about 5,000 million years, so we are quite safe at present!

Stardeath

Once a star like the Sun becomes a red giant, it is nearing the end of its life. The thin outer gas layers of the red giant star slowly drift off into space, forming a beautiful smoke-ring effect. Many such stellar smoke rings, such as the colorful Ring Nebula in the constellation Lyra, are visible in telescopes. These objects are termed planetry nebulas because they resemble the rounded disk of a planet.

At the center of a planetry nebula, the core of the former red giant is left behind, forming a tiny, hot star known as a white dwarf.

A red giant may be 100 times larger than the present-day Sun but a white dwarf is 100 times smaller than the Sun—that is, about the size of the Earth. To form such a tiny ball, the material must be densely compressed and a spoonful of matter from a white dwarf would weigh 10 tons.

Over billions of years, the white dwarf cools off, fading into invisibility, the end point in the evolution of a star like the Sun.

How long a star lives depends on how heavy it is. Stars smaller and cooler than the Sun live the longest, whereas bigger, hotter stars burn out more quickly than the Sun. For instance, the bright star Sirius, which is more than twice as heavy as the Sun, can live for only about 1,000 million years, one tenth the Sun's predicted total lifetime. Had Sirius been born at the same time as the Sun, it would already have burned out.

The heaviest stars of all, those at least four or five times the weight of the Sun, die in spectacular fashion. After such a star becomes a red giant, it erupts in a nuclear holocaust known as a supernova. For a few weeks or months the star's brightness increases billions of times as it throws off its outer layers into space. The famous Crab nebula (right), in the constellation Taurus, is the shattered remains of a star which astronomers saw erupt as a supernova in the year 1054.

A star does not always destroy itself entirely in a supernova. Sometimes the star's core is left behind, compressed into an object even smaller and denser than a white dwarf. Such a tiny super-dense object is termed a neutron star and is 1,000 times smaller than a white dwarf. A spoonful from it would weigh 1,000 million tons.

Neutron stars are so small and faint as to be almost invisible, but they give themselves away to astronomers on Earth because they emit strong pulses of radio waves. Each time the neutron star spins, about once a second on average, it gives out a flash of radio waves, rather like the beam from a lighthouse. Radio-flashing neutron stars are known as pulsars. Over 300 of them have been detected.

If the object left behind after a supernova weighs more than about three Suns, it is destined to become something even more extraordinary than a neutron star. The inward pull of the object's own gravity is so great that it begins to shrink until it has shrunk out of sight, becoming what is known as a black hole. Nothing can escape from the gravitational field of a black hole, not even the star's own light, so that it is completely invisible. However, things can fall into a black hole.

Black holes therefore act like a bottomless drain in the Universe. Gas plunging into a black hole heats up to many millions of degrees and emits short-wavelength radiation known as X rays. Astronomers have detected X rays which they believe come from hot gas falling into black holes in space.

Special Stars

Not all stars are as well behaved in their light output as the Sun. Some stars flicker in brightness, regularly or irregularly, over periods of days, weeks, or even years. They are known as variable stars.

Red giants are among the most common type of variable star. Being so big, they are unstable in size and brightness, flickering erratically over periods of months or years.

The most important type of variable stars are those which swell and contract regularly in size every few days. Their brightness varies regularly as a result of their changes in size. Such stars are named Cepheid variables after the first of the sort to be discovered, Delta Cephei.

The longer a Cepheid variable takes to go through its cycle of light changes, the brighter it is. Astronomers can therefore calculate the brightness by measuring the star's period of variation. The apparent brightness of a star is affected by its distance, so, by comparing a Cepheid variable's calculated brightness with its observed brightness, astronomers can tell the distance of the star and other stars around it. In this way, Cepheid variables are important distance indicators in space.

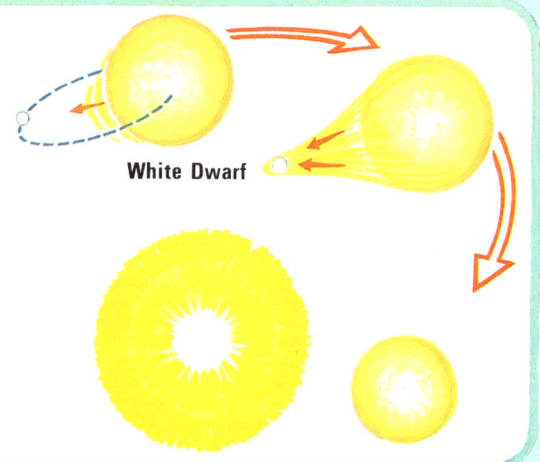

Some stars flare up temporarily to become thousands of times brighter, so that astronomers on Earth see a star where none had been visible before. These stars are termed novas, from the Latin meaning "new", although we now realize that they are not new at all. A nova is believed to occur in a double star system in which one star is a white dwarf. Gas flows from the companion star on to the white dwarf, causing it to flare up in brilliance. Unlike a supernova, the star does not blow itself to bits, and in fact novas can erupt several times in succession. Novas do not become as bright as supernovas.

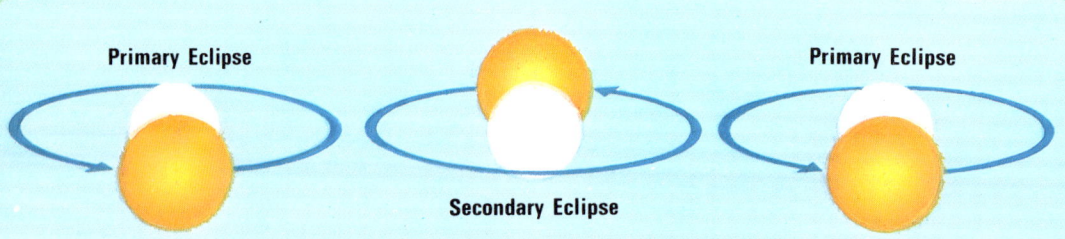

In some double star systems, one star periodically moves in front of the other as seen from Earth, thereby eclipsing it. When this happens, the total light we see from the system drops temporarily.

Such stars are known as eclipsing binaries. They come under the heading of variable stars, even though the stars themselves do not really change in brightness at all.

A famous eclipsing binary star is Algol, in the constellation Perseus. It consists of a faint yellow star and a bright blue one. Algol's light drops noticeably every 69 hours as the fainter star eclipses the brighter one.

Most stars are not alone like the Sun, but exist in groups of two, three or even more. These are known as double and multiple stars.

Double star systems can be extraordinary. In some cases, the stars are so close to each other that they are distorted by each other's gravity, and hot gas flows from one to another or even spirals off into space.

The stars of a double or multiple system can be very different from each other in size, brightness and color. For instance, the star Zeta Aurigae consists of a red giant orbited by a small blue star. If any planets exist in such a star system, the view from their surfaces would be spectacular.

The Milky Way

Our Sun is just one of more than 100,000 million stars that make up the vast star system known as the Galaxy.

If we could view our Galaxy from far away, we would see it as a spiral of stars, 100,000 light years in diameter and 2,000 light years thick.

All the stars we see in the night sky are relatively close to us in the Galaxy – mostly within about 1,000 light years. The more distant stars of the Galaxy form a faint, hazy band of light that we can see crossing the sky on dark nights. This band is called the Milky Way. When we look at the Milky Way we are actually looking through the thickest part of our Galaxy. Telescopes show that the Milky Way is made up of myriad faint stars seemingly crowded upon each other.

The name Milky Way is often used as an alternative title for the whole of the Galaxy.

A plan and side view of the Milky Way. The Sun (arrowed) lies about 30,000 light years from the center in one of the Galaxy's star-studded spiral arms. Astronomers can, of course, never see the Galaxy like this but they can calculate its size and shape by comparing their observations with those of other Galaxies.

Until about 50 years ago, astronomers thought that our Galaxy and the stars within it were all that existed in the entire Universe. Then, in the 1920s, the American astronomer Edwin Hubble showed that there were other galaxies far outside our own.

The first object he identified as another galaxy was a fuzzy patch which is just visible to the naked eye in the constellation Andromeda. Using the 100-inch reflecting telescope on Mount Wilson in California, Hubble found that this fuzzy patch was actually made up of faint stars far off in space.

The object is now known as the Andromeda galaxy. Latest measurements place the Andromeda galaxy at a distance of 2.2 million light years from us, which means that we see it as it appeared 2.2 million years ago. It is the most distant object visible to the naked eye.

The Andromeda galaxy is a spiral galaxy, similar in size and shape to our own Milky Way system. On the scale of the Universe, it is one of our closest neighbors. Hubble found many other galaxies scattered like islands throughout space. He classified them into various types, depending on their

A barred spiral galaxy

A lenticular galaxy

A spiral galaxy

shapes. Over half the known galaxies are spirals, like the Milky Way and the Andromeda galaxy (above). One quarter of all known galaxies are termed barred spirals. These differ from normal spirals in having a bar of stars across their centers. Most of the remaining galaxies are elliptical in shape. They are like flattened balls, with no spiral arms. A small percentage of galaxies, termed irregulars, have no particular shape at all. Examples of the irregular type of galaxy are the Magellanic Clouds, two small satellite galaxies of our Milky Way.

As the astronomer Edwin Hubble looked ever deeper into space, he made an astounding discovery. He found that the galaxies appeared to be moving apart from each other at high speed. This meant that the entire Universe must be expanding, like a balloon being blown up.

Hubble's discovery of the expansion of the Universe forms the basis of cosmology, the study of the origin and evolution of the Universe.

Origin of the Universe

How did the Universe begin? We may never know for sure, but here are the three main theories.

After Edwin Hubble discovered in the 1920s that the Universe was expanding, the Belgian astronomer Georges Lemaitre suggested that the Universe had begun in a massive explosion called the Big Bang. According to Lemaitre, all the matter in the Universe was once compressed together in one spot, and was sent flying outwards by the Big Bang explosion. Individual galaxies represent the lumps thrown out by the explosion. According to this theory, the Big Bang marks the origin of the Universe as we know it, although the cause of the explosion, and what happened before it, is a mystery.

If the motions of the galaxies are traced backwards, astronomers can work out when they were all crammed together. According to modern measurements of the speed of expansion of the Universe, the Big Bang must have occurred between 10,000 million and 20,000 million years ago.

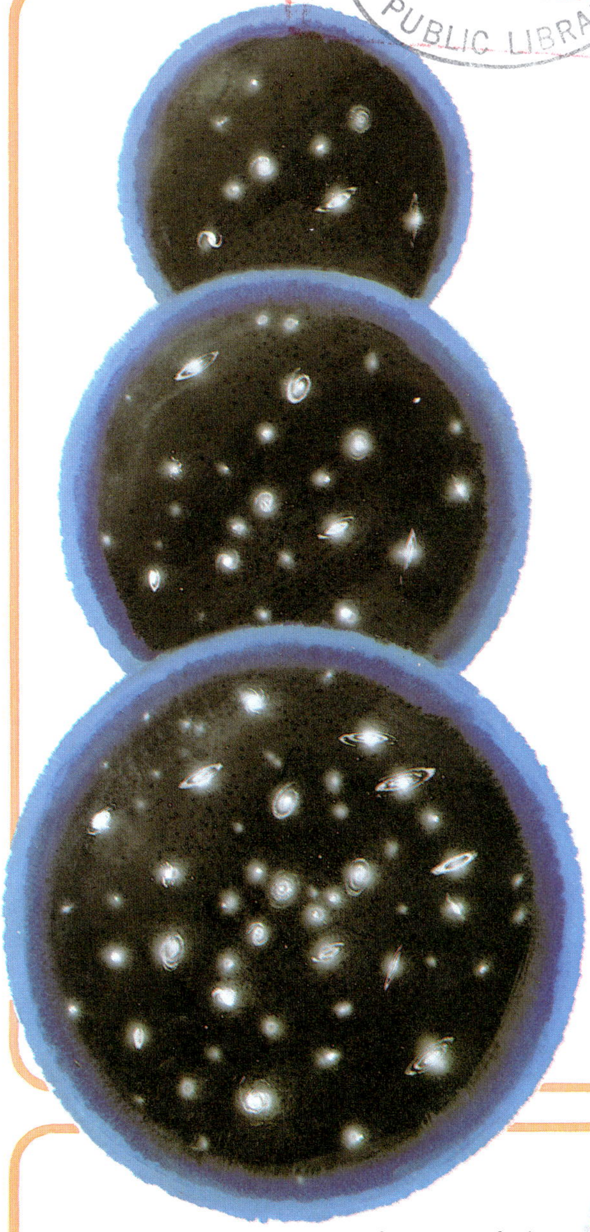

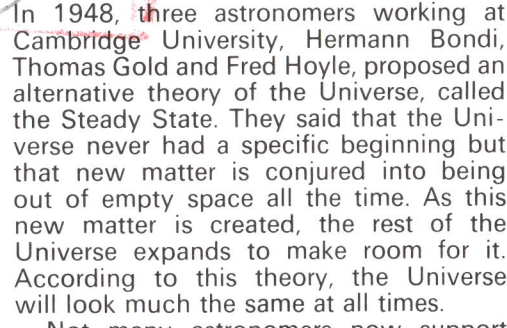

In 1948, three astronomers working at Cambridge University, Hermann Bondi, Thomas Gold and Fred Hoyle, proposed an alternative theory of the Universe, called the Steady State. They said that the Universe never had a specific beginning but that new matter is conjured into being out of empty space all the time. As this new matter is created, the rest of the Universe expands to make room for it. According to this theory, the Universe will look much the same at all times.

Not many astronomers now support this theory, for two main reasons. First, astronomers looking deep into space have found that the Universe appeared very different in the past, in contradiction of the Steady State theory but as predicted by the Big Bang. In particular, flaring objects known as quasars have been found far off in space. So distant are these objects that their light has taken billions of years to reach us, and so we see them as they appeared early in the history of the Universe. Quasars are believed by many astronomers to represent young galaxies in the process of formation. There are no quasars around today so they must have all evolved into galaxies as the Universe has grown older.

The second piece of evidence against the Steady State theory is that astronomers seem to have detected traces of the Big Bang explosion itself. Astronomers have found that space is not entirely cold, but is filled with a gentle warmth. This is believed to be heat left over from the incandescent fireball of the Big Bang.

A third theory is a modification of the Big Bang. It is known as the Oscillating Universe theory. This says that the Universe continually expands and contracts in cycles; the current expansion will eventually slow down and stop, to be replaced by contraction to another Big Bang, setting the process off again.

There is no sign that the expansion of the Universe will ever stop. According to current evidence, the Universe will continue to expand for ever, gradually thinning out until all the stars have died and eternal darkness descends.

How we Know

Astronomers study the sky with telescopes. A telescope collects more light than the human eye, allowing us to see objects much fainter than would otherwise be visible. The largest telescopes in the world can show stars and galaxies ten million times fainter than visible to the naked eye. Telescopes can also magnify objects, making them seem much closer to us.

There are two main types of telescope—refractors and reflectors. A refracting telescope collects light with a lens, like a spyglass or binoculars. Reflecting telescopes use a main mirror instead of a lens.

No one really knows who invented the first telescope, but the credit is usually given to the Dutch optician, Hans Lippershey, in 1609. He built a refractor using spectacle lenses. The Italian scientist Galileo heard of the invention and built one of his own. With this he began to study the sky, discovering the craters of the Moon, the satellites of Jupiter and the phases of Venus. His telescope was not very powerful and worked no better than modern binoculars.

In 1668 the English scientist Isaac Newton designed and built the first reflecting telescope. The largest telescopes in the world today are all reflectors, because mirrors are cheaper and easier to make than big

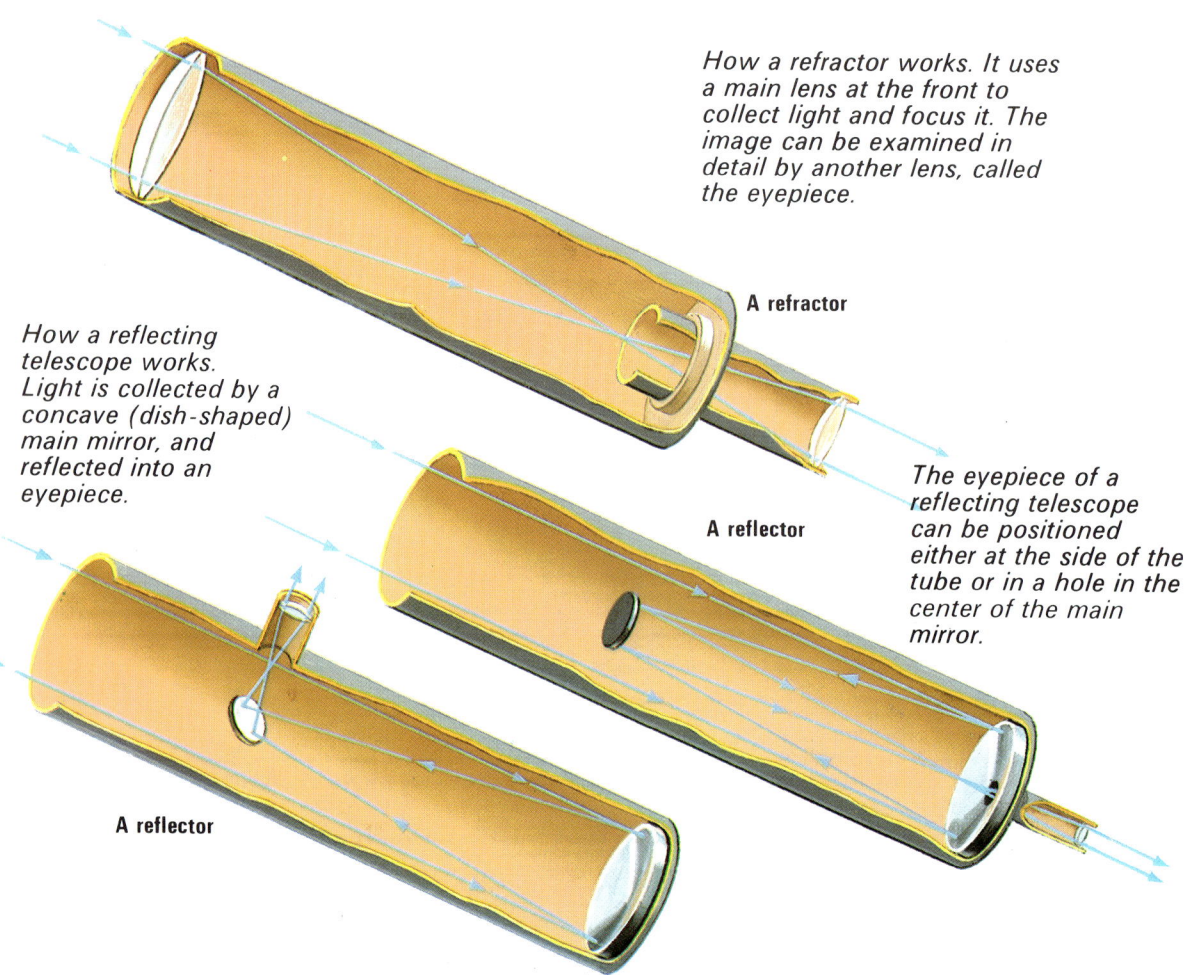

How a refractor works. It uses a main lens at the front to collect light and focus it. The image can be examined in detail by another lens, called the eyepiece.

A refractor

How a reflecting telescope works. Light is collected by a concave (dish-shaped) main mirror, and reflected into an eyepiece.

A reflector

The eyepiece of a reflecting telescope can be positioned either at the side of the tube or in a hole in the center of the main mirror.

A reflector

lenses. The world's largest refractor at the Yerkes Observatory in Wisconsin, has a main lens 40 inches in diameter. The world's largest reflector, in the Soviet Union, has a mirror 20 feet in diameter. Another large reflector is the 200-inch telescope on Palomar Mountain in California.

Modern telescopes are housed in giant buildings called observatories which are usually placed on top of high mountains to give a clear view of the sky.

Astronomers often use telescopes to take long-exposure photographs of the sky. A picture exposed for several hours can show objects that are usually too faint to be seen.

The Mount Palomar telescope

In the 1930s, scientists discovered that objects in space give out radio noise as well as light. Radio waves are similar to light waves, except that the waves are much longer and our eyes are not sensitive to them. Radio waves from space can be picked up by radio telescopes.

A radio telescope usually consists of a large dish which collects radio waves and focuses them on to a receiver. The radio noise is then amplified by electronic circuits, like a much more powerful form of domestic radio receiver. The biggest single radio dish in the world sits in a hollow between mountains at Arecibo, Puerto Rico. It is 1,000 feet in diameter.

A Saturn V rocket

Rockets

We are no longer restricted to making observations of the Universe from the surface of the Earth. Now, thanks to the development of the rocket, we can go into space.

Rockets are believed to have been invented by the Chinese over 750 years ago. Their rockets were like fireworks, with gunpowder as the fuel. Most modern rockets use liquid fuels but their principle of operation is the same as a firework.

Inside a rocket, fuel is burned to produce hot gas. The force of this gas escaping at high speed pushes the rocket along.

Usual fuels for modern rockets are kerosene or liquid hydrogen. Fuel cannot burn without oxygen and there is no oxygen in airless space. So a rocket carries its own supply of oxygen, also in liquid form.

The American rocket pioneer Robert H. Goddard built and flew the world's first liquid-fueled rocket in 1926 but it did not go very far. Much bigger rockets, called the V 2, were designed by Wernher von Braun for the German army during World War II. The V 2 could carry a one-ton payload a distance of 200 miles. After the war, von Braun and his colleagues moved to the USA where they continued work on rockets for space research. Here, von Braun designed the world's largest rocket, the Saturn V which took men to the Moon.

How can we get into space? To break away from the Earth's gravity which holds us down, we must go very quickly indeed.

Imagine throwing a ball into the air. It rises a little before falling back. If you throw the ball faster, it goes higher before falling back again. If it were possible to throw it at a speed of 5 miles a second, it would go into orbit around the Earth, becoming an artificial satellite. Artificial satellites orbit at heights of about 100 miles or more, above most of the atmosphere.

Large rockets can reach the high speeds necessary to put an object into orbit around the Earth. To escape the clutches of the Earth's gravity completely and move off into space, the rocket must go faster still.

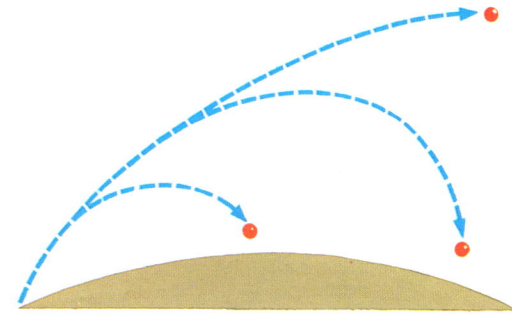

A ball would have to be thrown at a speed of 5 miles a second to put it into orbit.

The speed needed to break free from the Earth is 7 miles a second. This is known as escape velocity.

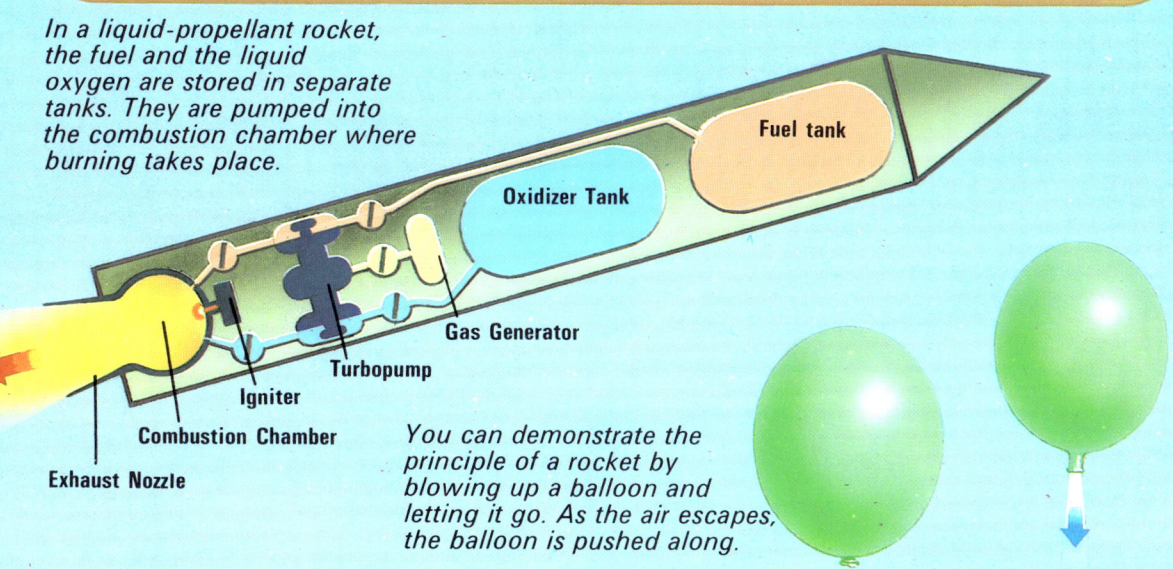

In a liquid-propellant rocket, the fuel and the liquid oxygen are stored in separate tanks. They are pumped into the combustion chamber where burning takes place.

You can demonstrate the principle of a rocket by blowing up a balloon and letting it go. As the air escapes, the balloon is pushed along.

Rockets are built in several sections, or stages, to help them reach the high speeds necessary to get into space. Each stage is a separate rocket, the bottom stage being the most powerful. This bottom stage begins to burn at launch and takes the rocket into the air. When each stage runs out of fuel, that section of the rocket falls away and the next stage takes over. Therefore the rocket gets lighter as it climbs higher. As a result, the rocket can go faster than if it were still carrying the unwanted weight of empty fuel tanks.

The stages of a rocket are usually stacked on top of each other but in some cases extra rockets can be added to the side of the first stage to give extra thrust at launch.

Rockets usually have two or three stages. The largest rocket ever built was the Saturn V which came in three stages. It was a total of 364 feet high and weighed 3,000 tons.

Satellites

A man-made object orbiting the Earth is known as an artificial satellite. Satellites are used for many purposes, from scientific research to military spying. Over 2,000 have been launched.

Satellites do not stay up in space for ever. They are gradually slowed down by the thin gases of the outer atmosphere until they fall back towards Earth. They are then burned up by friction but sometimes pieces of a satellite survive and crash on Earth like man-made meteorites.

Sputnik 1, the satellite that began the space age.

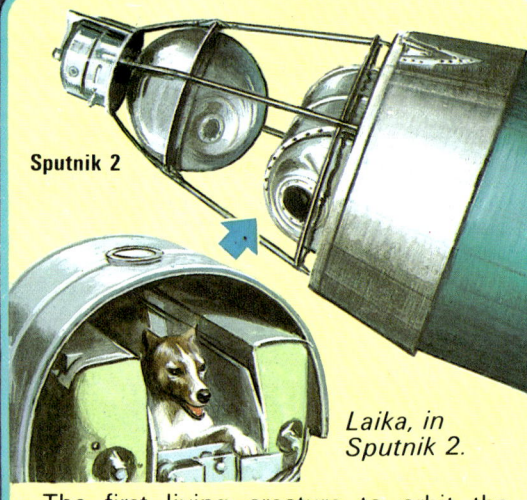

Sputnik 2

Laika, in Sputnik 2.

The first satellite to be put into orbit was Sputnik 1. It was launched by the Soviet Union on October 4, 1957. This date marked the start of the Space Age. Sputnik 1 was a sphere 23 inches in diameter with long radio antennas. It sent out radio signals so that scientists could track it as it went around the Earth. It re-entered the atmosphere after 3 months.

The first living creature to orbit the Earth was a female dog, Laika. She traveled in a special compartment of Sputnik 2, launched in November 1957. Laika died in space as there was no way to bring her back.

Satellites in space can see the Earth very clearly. Some satellites are designed to photograph clouds and to measure temperatures in the atmosphere, to help meteorologists make better weather forecasts. The first such weather satellite, Tiros 1, was launched in 1960. Now, several types of weather satellite orbit the Earth at various heights. The pictures they send back have helped to save lives by giving advanced warning of hurricanes in tropical areas.

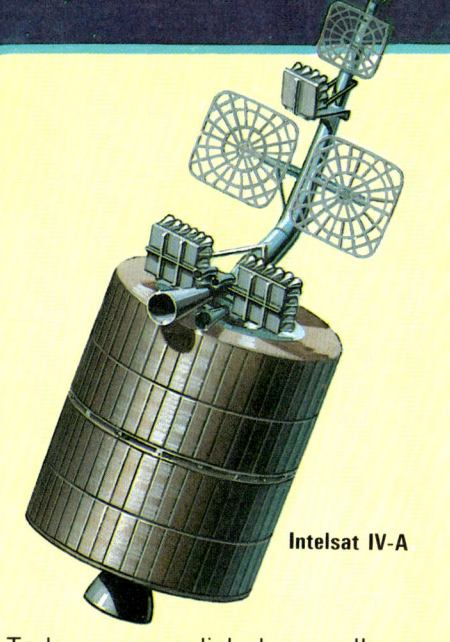

Intelsat IV-A

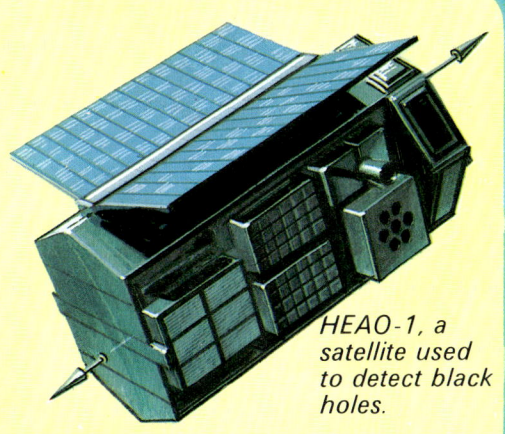

HEAO-1, a satellite used to detect black holes.

Today, we can dial phone calls around the world or see live TV pictures from the other side of the Earth thanks to communications satellites. An early satellite was Telstar, which relayed the first live TV pictures across the Atlantic from the USA to Europe. Modern communications satellites are stationed high above the Atlantic, Pacific and Indian Oceans to give world-wide coverage. Signals are sent to and from the satellites via ground stations like radio telescopes. The type of satellite shown here, Intelsat IV-A, can carry 9,000 telephone calls at a time. Even bigger satellites are now coming into use.

Astronomers use satellites to study the Universe. Above the atmosphere, the sky can be seen far more clearly than from the Earth. Satellites can detect radiation that does not get through the atmosphere, such as ultra-violet and X-rays. Several observatory satellites have been launched to find out more about the Sun, stars and galaxies. Some satellites are believed to have detected X rays emitted by hot gas falling into black holes.

The surface of the Earth can be surveyed from orbit more quickly and cheaply than from the ground or from an aircraft. Photographs taken by Earth-survey satellites reveal surprising detail that might otherwise be missed. Geologists use these photographs to look for areas in which new deposits of valuable minerals may be found. Some countries use pictures from Earth-survey satellites for map-making. Satellite photographs can show up areas of pollution in the atmosphere or ocean and areas of diseased crops.

Landsat

Space Probes

Space probes are robot explorers sent to study the Moon and planets. No life has been found on any planet, and all the planets have proved to be too hostile for humans to live on without protection. Because space probes are expendable, and can be made far more durable than a human, they can be sent to places where astronauts could never go, such as towards the surface of the Sun or through the radiation belts of Jupiter. All the planets out as far as Saturn have been reached by space probes. One of the two Voyager probes currently exploring the outer solar system is expected to reach Uranus in 1986 and Neptune in 1989.

The first space probes were sent towards the Moon, because it is the closest object to us in space. In September 1959, the Soviet probe Luna 2 became the first man-made object to hit the Moon (Luna 1 had missed), although it was destroyed on impact. More spectacular was Luna 3, which in October 1959 flew behind the Moon and radioed back the first photographs of the Moon's far side, which is always turned away from Earth.

To prepare for its series of Apollo manned lunar landings, the USA sent two series of space probes to the Moon. One series was called Surveyor, which landed automatically on the surface to prove it was safe for men to follow. The other probes were called Lunar Orbiter which orbited the Moon and photographed its entire surface, spying out suitable landing sites for the Apollo missions.

The Soviet Union has used robot craft to bring back small samples of soil automatically from the Moon. They have also developed another type of craft, called Lunokhod, which was driven around on the surface of the Moon by remote control from Earth.

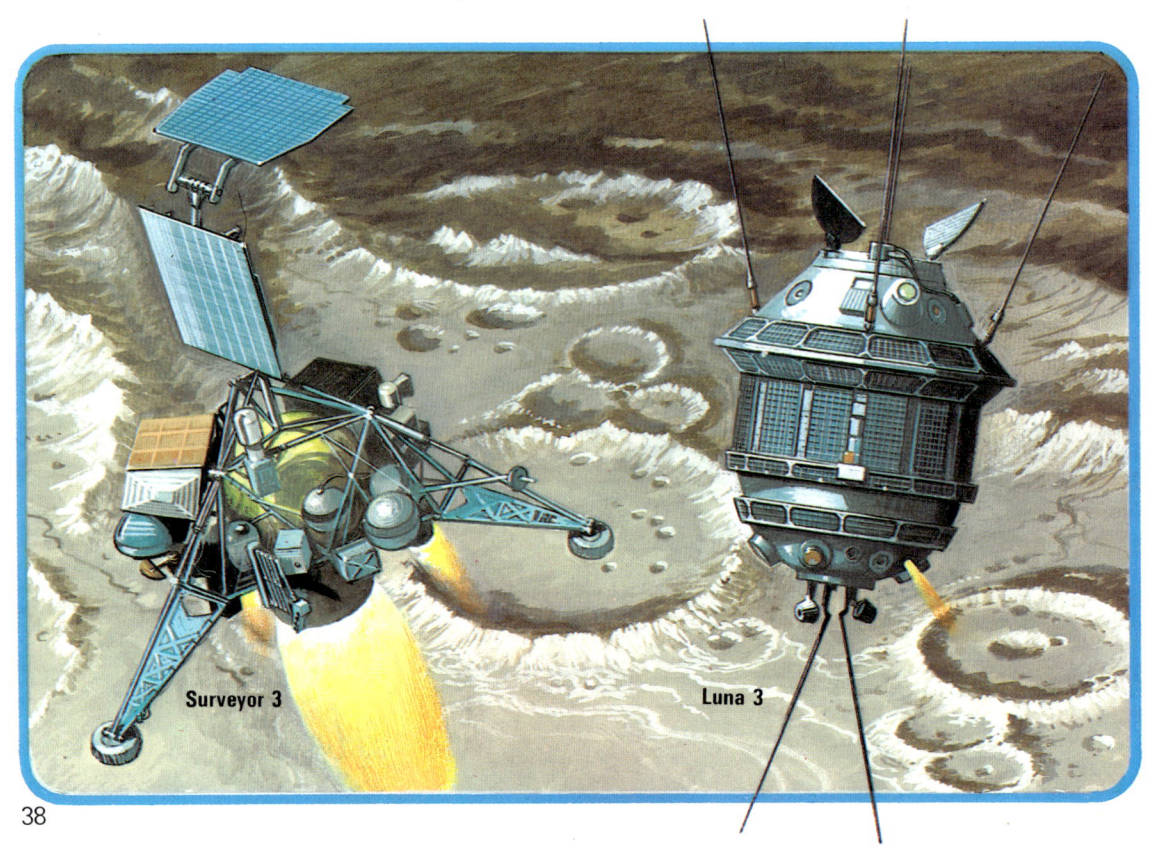

Lunokhod

The first probe to reach another planet was the American Mariner 2, which flew past Venus in 1962. The Soviet Union has shown great interest in the exploration of Venus and have parachuted probes down through the planet's atmosphere which have sent back information and photographs.

Other American Mariner probes have photographed Mercury and Mars, and, in 1979, one of the most difficult feats of the space age was successfully achieved when two Viking space probes landed automatically on Mars. The Viking landers tested for signs of life on Mars but found none.

The giant planets Jupiter and Saturn have recently come under the attention of space probes. They were first photographed by American probes of the Pioneer series, followed by two more advanced probes called Voyager. In future, probes will be sent to orbit Jupiter and to sample its atmosphere.

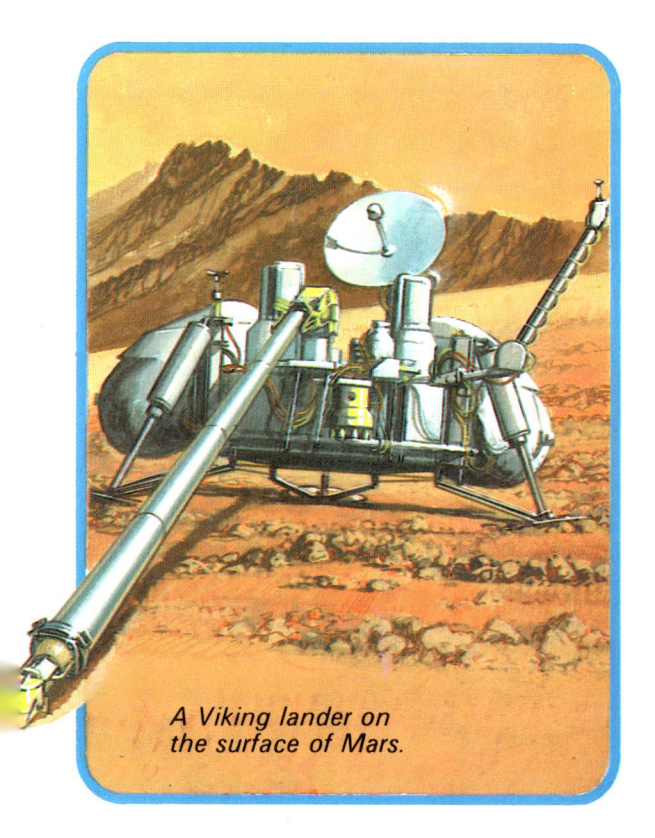

A Viking lander on the surface of Mars.

A Pioneer probe flying past Jupiter.

Man in Space

Putting a human being into space is more difficult than orbiting a satellite. To keep the occupant alive in the airlessness of space, a spacecraft must carry supplies of air and be sealed to stop the air escaping. It must have electricity to power the systems on board and must also carry food and water for the astronaut. The temperature must be kept at a comfortable level, and to return safely to Earth, the spacecraft must have a heat shield to protect it from burning up during re-entry through the atmosphere.

Yuri Gagarin, the first man in space, orbited the Earth in Vostok 1 on April 12, 1961.

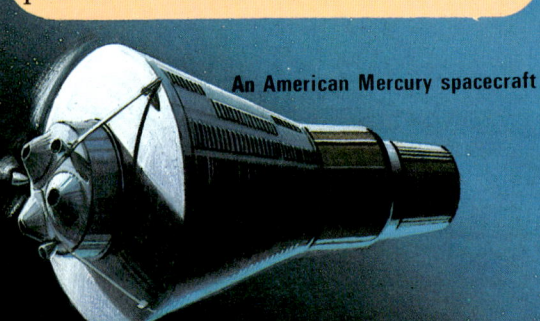

An American Mercury spacecraft

A Vostok spacecraft

American astronauts made their first "walks" in space from the two-man Gemini Spacecraft in 1965.

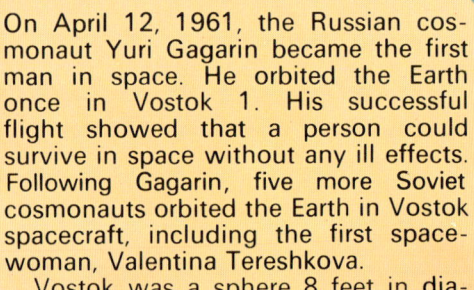

On April 12, 1961, the Russian cosmonaut Yuri Gagarin became the first man in space. He orbited the Earth once in Vostok 1. His successful flight showed that a person could survive in space without any ill effects. Following Gagarin, five more Soviet cosmonauts orbited the Earth in Vostok spacecraft, including the first spacewoman, Valentina Tereshkova.

Vostok was a sphere 8 feet in diameter and a later modified version, Voskhod, carried two and sometimes three men into space at once. One cosmonaut, Alexei Leonov, crawled out of his spacecraft through a hatch to make the first "walk" in space.

The first American spaceman, John Glenn, flew in a single-seat, cone-shaped capsule called Mercury in 1962. This was followed by larger craft called Gemini which housed two men.

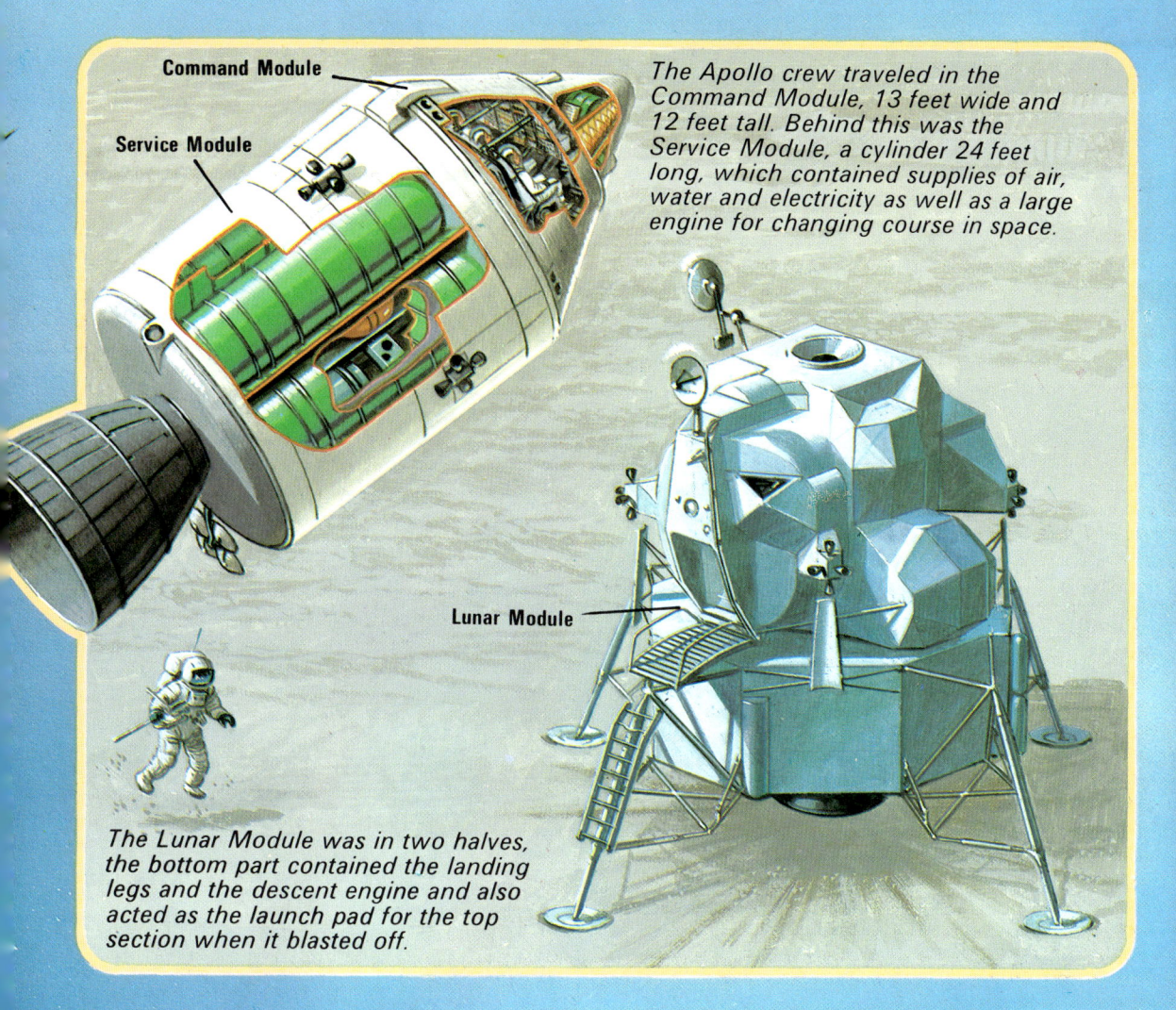

Command Module

Service Module

The Apollo crew traveled in the Command Module, 13 feet wide and 12 feet tall. Behind this was the Service Module, a cylinder 24 feet long, which contained supplies of air, water and electricity as well as a large engine for changing course in space.

Lunar Module

The Lunar Module was in two halves, the bottom part contained the landing legs and the descent engine and also acted as the launch pad for the top section when it blasted off.

The American Mercury and Gemini programmes paved the way for the Apollo missions which took astronauts to the Moon. Apollo was launched towards the Moon by the world's largest rocket, the Saturn V. Apollo was a three-man craft. The crew traveled in the Command Module which sat on top of the Service Module. The whole Apollo spacecraft weighed about 30 tons.

Under the Command and Service Modules was stored the Lunar Module, the spidery craft which would actually touch down on the Moon. Once on the way to the Moon, the Apollo astronauts turned the Command and Service Modules and docked with the Lunar Module. Two astronauts crawled through a docking tunnel into the Lunar Module. When safely in orbit around the Moon, they descended to the surface in the Lunar Module. Astronauts Neil Armstrong and Edwin Aldrin made the first Moon landing on July 20 1969 on the Apollo 11 mission.

There were many Apollo missions and Apollo capsules were also used to take astronauts to the Skylab space station orbiting the Earth. In 1975, an Apollo capsule docked in orbit with a Soviet spacecraft called Soyuz.

In the future, there may be more joint space missions between the East and West.

Space Stations

To live and work in space for long periods, astronauts need more room than available in ordinary spacecraft. Large space stations have therefore been launched that are capable of housing a crew for several months.

Skylab, an American space station, was the largest object put into orbit, 82 feet long, it weighed 75 tons. It was the converted top stage of a Saturn V rocket and was launched on May 14, 1973. During the launch it was damaged. A panel covered with solar cells which turn sunlight into electricity, was torn off and another panel was jammed, so that the station was short of electrical power. Also torn off was a shield intended to screen the station from the Sun's rays. Without this shield, Skylab began to overheat.

The first crew to go up to Skylab had to carry out running repairs. The astronauts cut free the jammed electricity panel and spread out a sunshade to protect Skylab from the Sun's heat. These repairs proved successful and the astronauts were able to begin work aboard the space station. Three crews traveled to Skylab and the third crew stayed for three months which was the endurance record at that time.

Skylab carried a battery of telescopes to study the Sun at short wavelengths that do not get through the atmosphere. It also had cameras and other equipment to survey the surface of the Earth.

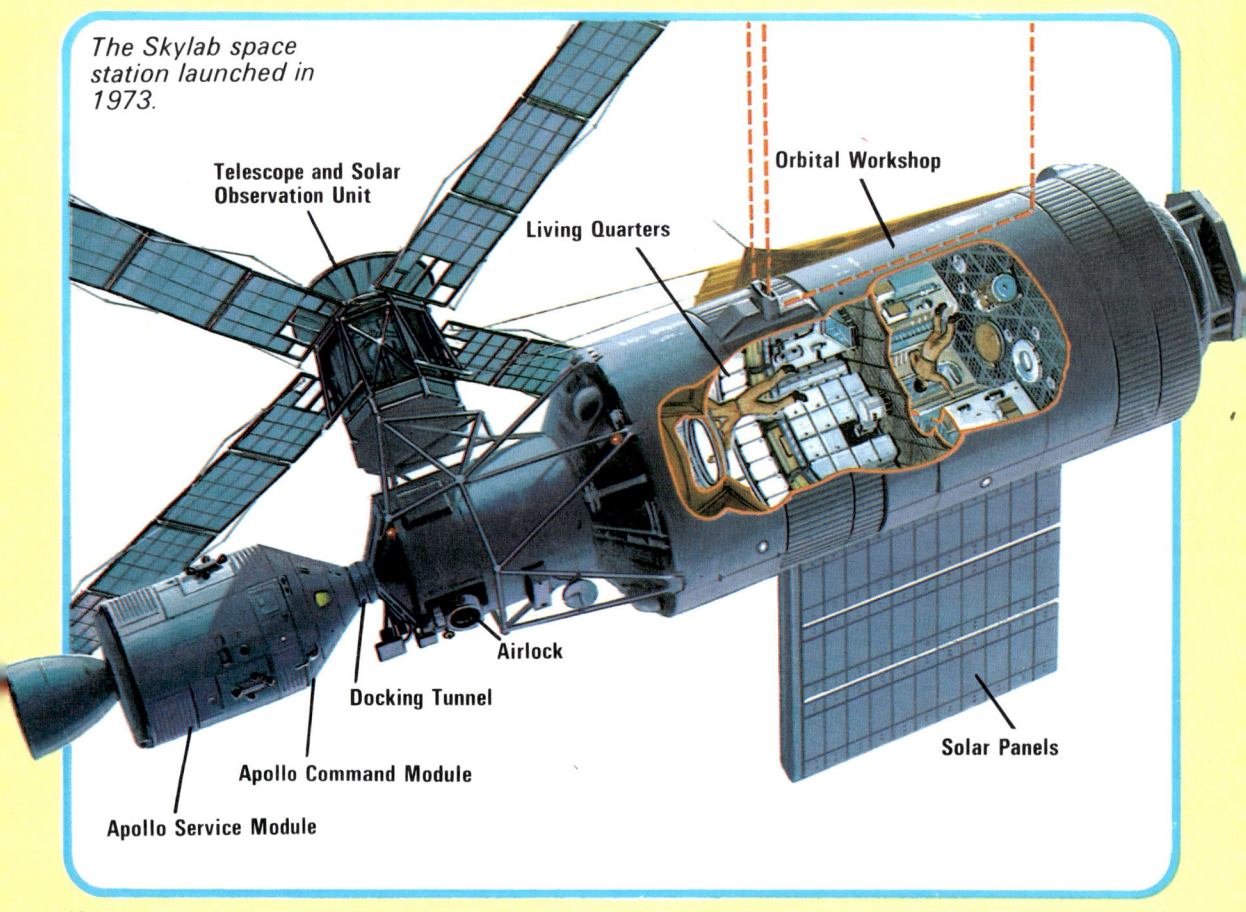

The Skylab space station launched in 1973.

The Soviet Union's space station, Salyut, in which cosmonauts set an endurance record of over five months in space.

The astronauts also studied the changes in their bodies over long periods in space. Everything in orbit is weightless because it is "falling" endlessly around the Earth. In weightlessness, an astronaut's heart, muscles and bones become weaker and there are changes in blood cells. To counteract these changes, astronauts must take lots of exercise while in space. Once back on Earth, the astronauts' bodies return to normal. Fortunately, no permanent changes to astronauts have resulted from spending long periods in space.

Weightlessness has certain uses. For instance, liquids that will not mix when under the influence of the Earth's gravity will mix successfully in weightlessness. Therefore, new types of metal and glass can be made in space that it would be impossible to produce on Earth.

After the final crew departed Skylab in 1974, the space station was abandoned. It re-entered the Earth's atmosphere in July 1979.

The Soviet Union has launched a series of space stations called Salyut, made from the modified top stage of a launch rocket. Salyut space stations are less than half the size of the American Skylab but the cosmonauts carried out similar experiments and set new endurance records, remaining in orbit for over five months.

Such extended missions show that men can survive in space long enough for a flight to Mars. In the future, permanently manned space stations may be set in orbit around the Earth or Moon.

New Era in Space

The introduction of the Space Shuttle has opened up a new era in spaceflight. Before the Shuttle, all rockets and manned spacecraft were used only once. After each mission they were scrapped, which made spaceflight very expensive. The Space Shuttle overcomes the problem. It is a combined launch rocket and manned spacecraft that can be recovered and reused many times. The Shuttle cuts the cost of spaceflight by up to 90%.

The Space Shuttle is launched by a rocket but glides back to land on a runway like an aircraft. The part of the Shuttle which actually goes into space is a winged craft the size of a jet airliner. This craft, known as the Orbiter, carries a crew of four or more. The Orbiter has three main engines which are fed with fuel from a large tank. Two extra rockets are attached at the sides to help boost the Shuttle at launch. As it climbs into the air, the extra rockets fall away, parachuting into the ocean, where they are recovered and can be later reused. Powered by its main engines, the Shuttle continues into orbit. The fuel tank is jettisoned and burns up.

The Orbiter can carry up to 29 tons into space in its large cargo bay. Several large satellites can be put into orbit at once, and old satellites, or those that need repair, can be brought back to Earth.

The Shuttle is designed to stay in orbit for up to a week at a time. When its mission is finished, it glides back through the atmosphere. Insulating tiles protect its outer surface from the heat of re-entry. After it has landed, the Shuttle Orbiter can be reloaded and launched again.

Spacelab is a space station built by the European Space Agency. It will be carried into orbit in the cargo bay of the Space Shuttle. Scientists from Europe and the USA will fly for a week or more in Spacelab, carrying out experiments in orbit. The space station consists of two parts. One part is a pressurized section in which the scientists can work in shirt sleeves, without the need for spacesuits. There is also a section open to the vacuum of space on which equipment can be mounted for observing the Earth and sky. Scientists aboard Spacelab will continue the work begun by the Skylab astronauts. Experiments on manufacturing in space aboard Spacelab could mark the start of whole new space industries.

Among the important cargoes to be launched by the Space Shuttle is the Space Telescope. This is a large reflector with a mirror 100 inches in diameter, far bigger than any telescope so far put into space. The Space Telescope will be able to see objects 100 times fainter, and detail 10 times smaller, than the largest telescopes on Earth.

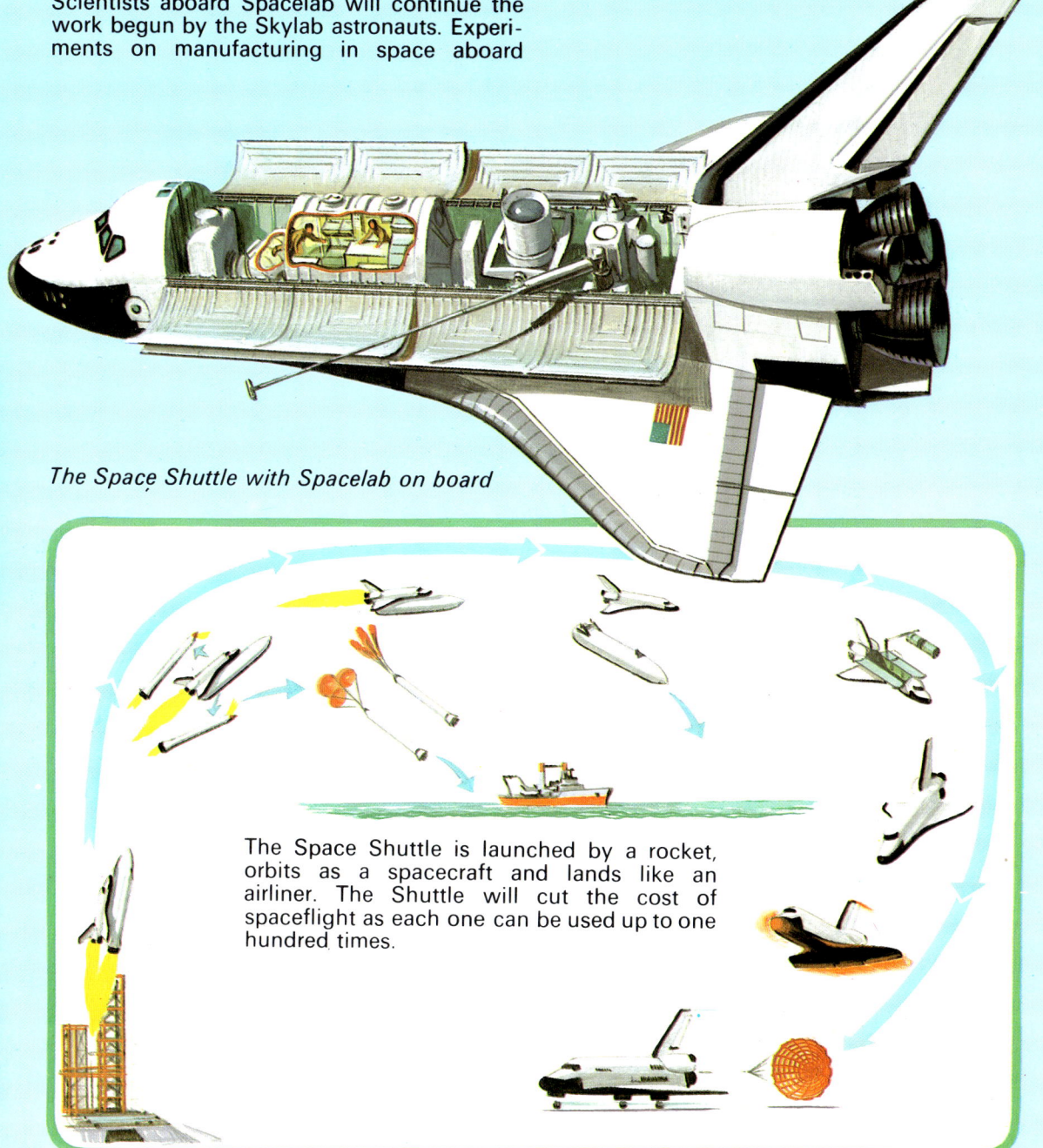

The Space Shuttle with Spacelab on board

The Space Shuttle is launched by a rocket, orbits as a spacecraft and lands like an airliner. The Shuttle will cut the cost of spaceflight as each one can be used up to one hundred times.

The Future

Future space stations will be much bigger than those of today, housing dozens of astronauts at a time. Next century, it may be possible to build giant space colonies with room for thousands of people. Such colonies would be spheres or cylinders, rotating to provide artificial gravity on their inner surfaces, where people live. The insides of the colonies would be landscaped to look as much like the Earth as possible.

Mirrors would reflect sunlight into the colonies through windows, and climate could be controlled by the amount of sunlight let in. The colonies would be completely self-contained, growing their own food and using solar power for energy.

Space colonies could be built from materials mined on the Moon. The first colonies will be set up in orbit around the Earth, but colonies could eventually be placed anywhere in the solar system. Millions of people could be living in space colonies next century.

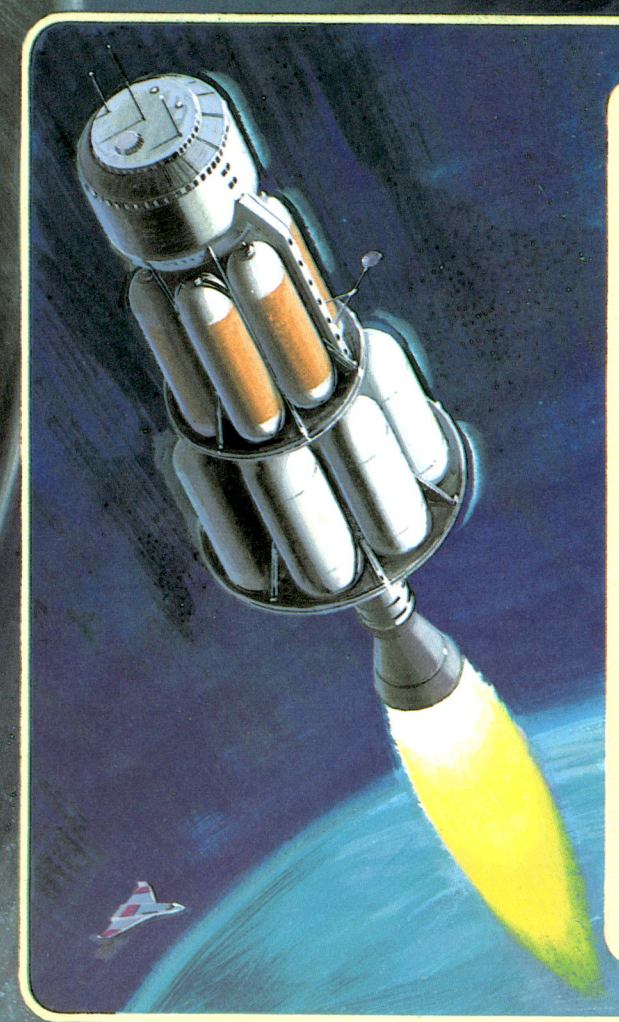

In the future, we should be able to send space probes to the stars, but they will require rockets far more powerful than available at present. The problem is that the stars are so far away; traveling at today's speeds, space probes would take 100,000 years to reach even the nearest star, Alpha Centauri. To reach the stars in a shorter time, we must develop new and faster rockets.

The first probes to set off for the stars will probably be powered by nuclear energy. One suggestion is for a two-stage craft propelled by the explosion of hydrogen bombs. These would be set off in a special chamber behind the craft, and the force of their blast would push it along. Such a starship could reach a top speed of 80 million mph and would take 50 years to reach the nearest stars. At the destination, probes would study the target star and any planets around it, radioing the information back to Earth.

Starships will be difficult to make and there are no plans to build one yet, but we might send probes to the stars next century. Not until robot explorers have scouted the nearest stars will astronauts follow.

Many scientists are interested in finding out whether there is life elsewhere in space. Some radio astronomers have begun to listen for possible radio messages from beings on planets around other stars.

Some people think that we are already being visited by aliens. They point to sightings of strange objects in the sky, often known as flying saucers but more correctly termed Unidentified Flying Objects (UFOs). Most UFOs turn out on identification to be misidentifications of natural or man-made objects such as stars, planets, satellites, or aircraft.

Index

Aldrin, Edwin 6, 41
Algol (in Perseus) 26
Alpha Centauri 4, 47
Andromeda 28, 29
Apollo 6, 38, 41
Arecibo (radio telescope) 33
Arcturus (in Boötes) 23
Arizona meteorite crater 18
Armstrong, Neil 6, 41
Asteroids 4, 5, 10, 18

Big Bang 30, 31
Black Hole 25, 37
Bondi, Hermann 31

Callisto 13
Cassini's division 15
Cepheid variable stars 27
Ceres 18
Comets 4, 5, 19, 39
Corona 20, 21
Crab Nebula (in Taurus) 25

Deimos 10
Delta Cepheid 26

Earth 4, 5, 6, 7, 8, 9, 10, 11, 12, 13, 18, 19, 20, 21, 23, 24, 25, 26, 34, 35, 36, 37, 38, 40, 41, 42, 43, 44, 45, 46, 47
Eclipse (of the Sun or Moon) 21
Eclipsing binaries 26
Escape velocity 35
Evening "star" 9

Flares 20

Gagarin, Yuri 40
Galaxy 23, 28, 29, 30
Galilei, Galileo 13, 15, 32
Ganymede 13
Gemini 40
Glenn, John 40
Goddard, Robert H. 34
Gold, Thomas 31
Grootfontein meteorite 18

Halley's comet 19
HEAO-1 37
Herschel, William 16
Hoyle, Fred 31
Hubble, Edwin 28, 29, 30

Intelsat IV-A 37
Io 13

Jupiter 4, 12, 13, 14, 18, 39

Laika 36
Landsat 37
Lemaitre, George 30
Leonov, Alexei 40
Light year 4
Lipphershey, Hans 32
Lowell, Percival 10
Luna 1 38
Luna 2 38
Luna 3 38
Lunokhod 38

Magellanic Clouds 29
Mariner 2 39
Mariner 10 8
Mars 4, 10, 11, 18, 39, 43
Mercury 4, 5, 8, 23, 39
Mercury (spacecraft) 40, 41

Meteorites 5, 7, 8, 11, 18
Meteors 19
Milky Way 28, 29
Moon 5, 6, 7, 8, 17, 21, 34, 38, 41, 43
Moons 5, 10, 13, 15, 16, 17
Morning "star" 9
Mount Wilson (telescope) 28

Neptune 4, 16, 17
Neutron Star 25
Newton, Isaac 32
Nova 26

Olympus Mons 11
Orion nebula 22
Oscillating Universe theory 31

Perseid meteros 19
Phases (of the Moon) 7
Phobos 10
Photosphere 20, 21
Pleiades 23
Pluto 4, 17
Prominence 20
Pulsars 25

Quasars 31

Radio telescope 33
Red Giant 22, 23, 26, 27
Red Spot 13
Reflector (telescope) 32, 33
Refractor (telescope) 32
Ring Nebula (in Lyra) 24
Rockets 34, 35, 47

Salyut 43
Satellites 35, 36, 37
Saturn 4, 14, 15, 39
Saturn V 34, 35, 41, 42
Sirius 25

Skylab 41, 42, 43
Solar system 4, 5, 6, 16, 17, 18, 19
Soyuz 41
Spacelab 45
Space shuttle 44, 45
Space Telescope 45
Sputnik 1 36
Sputnik 2 36
Starship 47
Steady State theory 31
Sun 4, 5, 7, 8, 9, 10, 12, 14, 16, 17, 18, 19, 20, 21, 22, 23, 24, 25, 26, 27, 37, 42
Sunspots 20, 21
Supernova 25, 26
Surveyor 3 38

Telescope 4, 28, 32, 33
Telstar 37
Tereshkova, Valentina 40
Tiros 1 36
Titan 15
Transit 8

UFOs 47
Uranus 4, 16

V2 34
Venus 4, 5, 9, 23, 39
Viking 10, 11, 39
von Braun, Wernher 35
Voskhod 40
Vostok 1 40
Voyager 13, 38, 39

White Dwarf 22, 24, 25, 26

X rays 25, 37

Yerkes Observatory 33

Zeta Aurigae 27